Collecting for Tomorrow

Kitchenware

THE
LILIAN S. BESORE
MEMORIAL LIBRARY
GREENCASTLE, PENNSYLVANIA
FOUNDED MARCH 20, 1963

D1412228

Collecting for Tomorrow

Kitchenware

Jo Marshall

CHILTON BOOK COMPANY
Radnor, Pennsylvania

First published in the USA in 1976, by The Chilton Book Co., Radnor, Pa. and simultaneously in Canada by Thomas Nelson & Sons, Ltd., Don Mills, Ontario.

Designed and produced by
Walter Parrish International Ltd., London

Made and printed in Great Britain by
Purnell and Sons Limited,
Paulton near Bristol, Avon, England

Library of Congress Catalog Card No.: 76-3225
ISBN 0-8019-6401-6

For Carolyn and Ann

Contents

Author's acknowledgements

I should like to thank Mr Evan Perry of Horsham Museum for his kind advice and permission to photograph a number of items in the Museum; Dr Bernard Watney for his help and information about corkscrews; Mr Christopher Sykes of Woburn and his two charming assistants; Mrs Irwin, Librarian of the American Museum at Bath; the Librarian of the Museum of Rural Life at Reading; and many librarians at reference libraries in London and Essex. My special thanks are due to my colleagues Mr Brian Cole, Mr John Matthews and Mr John Sandon; also to the people who have kindly given us permission to photograph, both here and in America; to Jane Maitland Hudson and Gilly Macmeeken, of Walter Parrish International, for their help and patience. A heartfelt word of thanks also to my family and friends for their forbearance while I have been buried in 'pots and pans'.

Introduction

To be able fully to appreciate the art of any period it is necessary to understand the social history of that time. It is possible that collectors of kitchenware will find articles of the late 17th and 18th centuries, but these will be rare. The 19th century will be the period providing the bulk of most collections, as it was a century of very great and very rapid change. The Industrial Revolution which started at the close of the 18th century brought a complete change of life-style in England and, later on, in America. They became industrial countries and Britain's dependence on foreign supplies of food became more and more marked as industrialisation advanced.

The advent of railways and steamships brought an end to isolation, both nationally and internationally. Improved methods of communication furthered this development. As Britain became more a producer of manufactured goods so her towns grew and people moved from the land. They moved also from a situation where they had been self-supporting to an extent, to a situation of dependence—in 1850 Britain imported only 25% of her grain, mainly from Russia; by 1881, almost two thirds of Britain's wheat and flour came from America. In America railways and steamships had cut both distance and freight costs and steam traffic had opened up the vast American prairies—they poured their wheat into eastern seaports for export.

A new element was introduced into diet by food preservation and refrigeration. After a number of inventions in icemaking in America, as early as 1810, the first freezing works in the world were started by Sutcliffe Mort in New South Wales, Australia, and in 1880 the first cargo of frozen mutton was brought to England in the *Strathleven*.

With the aid of refrigeration plants on trains and steamers, the Chicago meat trade increased at a phenomenal rate. At the end of the 19th century, it was easier to put Australian food on English tables in perfect condition than it had been to put French or Irish produce there when Queen Victoria was on the throne.

The needs of an expanding population and a rising standard of living made the production of more food and manufactured goods imperative. Science invaded the kitchen and the proliferation of tables, nutritional indexes, and 'domestic science' instead of 'housewifery' began. On the title page a recipe book published in 1862 is described as the 'Dictionary of practical recipies, containing the arcana of trade and manufacturing, domestic economy, artistical, ornamental and scientific processes, pharmaceutical and chemical preparations . . .' In 1863 the Privy Council instituted the first national inquiry into diet—an important landmark in the history of food and health.

There was little or no protection against polluted water, no adequate sewage arrangements and little or no protection against putrefying meat or rancid flour. It would be difficult for the modern housewife to imagine a kitchen lit by evil-smelling and smoking oil lamps or tallow candles, her heat and means of cooking coming from an open fire with perhaps an oven beside it, no piped water, no hot water, no drainage. Yet in spite of all these difficulties, the kitchen was the 'factory' of the household—although even in 1893 Mrs. Kellogg in her book *Science in the Kitchen* said: 'It is a mistake to suppose that any room however small and unpleasantly situated is "good enough" for a kitchen. This is the room where housekeepers pass a great portion of their time and it should be one of the brightest and most convenient rooms in the house.'

The housewife, even in well-to-do and wealthy households, would herself, or expect her servants to, pickle and preserve meat hams and tongues, salt beef, dry herbs, make preserves, prepare sausages. In 1845, Eliza Acton in her book *Modern Cookery,* starts her recipe for Roast Sucking Pig as follows: 'After the pig has been scalded and prepared for the spit'. She also gives a number of recipes for 'store sauces', meaning sauces made for the store cupboard. Such house-wives often made their own wines and beers and there are recipes for such intriguing brews as 'surfeit water, hysterical water, clary water and saffron cordial'. The housewife would have been the doctor for her family on most occasions and there are known recipes for 'angelica water which wonderfully strengthens the heart' and 'rose-mary water which is an excellent cephalic and stomachic'!

To us, the most interesting aspect of the sudden increase in various kinds of foods is the equally profuse explosion of new gadgets and utensils in Victorian times. Mass-manufacturing meant cheap prices, mass food production meant hundreds of new proces-ses and foods, each needing equipment and implements.

Most kitchenware collectors begin with an avid interest in cooking, and domestic books of all kinds provide the source of much of our knowledge of utensils and their dates. Look for lists of utensils, often put at the beginning of recipe books—you will find surprisingly modern ideas together with some that will sound very ancient!

One such chapter in an American ice cream book of 1886 includes a strainer, egg beater, lemon squeezer, lactometer, and a sacchorometer—all very familiar today. But there is also a mortar and pestle, a large boxwood spoon, an ice 'cane', and, mentioned with special pride, a glass graduated measure.

Cross check with such books, old magazines, manufacturers' advertisements in contemporary papers—all these are a mine of information.

Yet, above all, the most tangible evidence we have of the day-to-day work in the kitchen lies in the utensils and equipment which have survived. I have tried to give some idea of the processes of cooking, cleaning, lighting, laundering, in past times, by the items we have illustrated. In the text, I have endeavoured to fill in some historical background and some hints on collecting. Collections of kitchenware will range over a number of materials—wood, various metals, pottery, porcelain, glass. The collector will find many products handmade by the small village craftsman and some factory-produced objects, some with makers' marks and others whose origins will never be known, and whose function remains equally obscure!

With the revival of natural foods and home-made dishes, there has been a growing fascination for the equipment used in the past. Some 'genuine antique' pots and pans, 'just like granny used' are obvious fakes, but some are not so obvious, and have found their way into junk shops and antique markets.

When items become collectable and of commercial value, there is always the danger of fakes and copies. However, with kitchenware it should always be remembered that the utensils and equipment were made for use, and will show signs of wear and having been cleaned over many years. As with all other forms of collecting there is no substitute for looking at and handling and getting the 'feel' of old materials.

Learn as much as you can about the use and manufacture of tin, iron, and copper in particular, since these were used so often in the kitchen. Buy damaged bits and pieces (very cheaply, of course!) to see how nuts and bolts worked, how spoons were cast, why tin cutters had a folded edge, and so forth. This will help enormously in judging better pieces.

Since kitchenware, particularly of the later period, is a fairly new field for the collector, it is impossible to give any idea at all of price. In general, follow the rule of all antiques—the older, the more expensive; anything that is incomplete loses its value quickly (so learn to look for details like replaced handles and newly added bits of machinery), as does damaged pottery or very rusty iron—rust is not just a dirty finish, it dissolves the iron itself. On the other hand, variety can overcome all these disadvantages, and if poor condition is only the need of soap and water or polish, then your time and trouble will probably get you a better buy than a beautifully polished and lacquered pan shining in an expensive dealer's window.

As far as gadgets and patented items of the 19th and early 20th centuries are concerned, there is a great deal of interesting research to be done which can add to the fun of hunting down pieces in shops, auction sales and even old houses about to be demolished.

Perhaps more than any other kind of collecting, kitchenware is enormously satisfying because it gives us insight into the daily life our families once knew. As George Meredith said: 'Kissing don't last—cookery do'.

Illumination in the kitchen

Before electricity people of moderate means used wax candles only for 'best occasions' and tallow dips for everyday use. Tallow candles were often made at home by dipping a wick into melted fat (usually bacon or mutton), letting it dry and then repeating the process until the candle was large enough. It must have been a tedious and messy business. Less expensive were rushlights, which were also made at home. These were set in holders, usually home-made too, and cut from wood, though some were made from iron and were set on a wooden block, with a movable 'jaw' to hold the rushlight. Other types of holders had sockets which held either candles or rushlights, yet others were tall and stood on the floor, and some were for use on the table. Candles had to be kept dry and in the 18th century they were sometimes kept in small chests with sliding lids. In the 19th century tubular tin holders with hanging straps were used.

Candle moulds were invented in the 15th century by Sieur de Brez. The candles were made by repeatedly dipping a fine wick into a vessel or pan of wax or tallow. Most candles were still made in this way until candle-making machines were invented in the 19th century.

Oil lamps have been used since ancient times. A significant development in design came in the 18th century when the wick was passed through a vertical tube in the top of the oil vessel. In the 19th century the rock-and-pin wick was introduced—previously the wick could only be raised with a spike or forceps. The 'crusie' lamp has been used in the Shetlands and Netherlands for the last 250 years—the lower pan catches the drips and surplus oil.

Candles or rushlights were lit either with a tinderbox or with a spill from the fire. The tinder-box contained a piece of flint, a steel and a small quantity of charred rag known as tinder. The edge of the flint hit the wheel obliquely, knocking off tiny particles which caused the tinder to smoulder; a sulphur match could then be lit from the glowing tinder.

Top, left to right: early-18th-century triple mould for tallow candles; 18th century rushlight holder with candle socket spiked into wooden block; 'crusie' lamp in hammered sheet iron, probably late 17th century (probably Scottish or French). Centre: 18th-century iron candle box. Bottom row, left to right: early-19th-century tinder box; 18th-century cast-iron tallow pan used in making rushlights.

Cooking for Royalty

The magnificent kitchen in the fantastic Royal Pavilion at Brighton gives some idea of what a large kitchen looked like in the early 19th century and shows that the methods of cooking had changed little over the centuries—meat, for instance, was still roasted on a spit in front of an open fire. The kitchen was built in 1816 and was much admired—J. W. Croker in his *Journal* for 1818/19 described it as follows: 'The kitchens and larders are admirable—such contrivances for roasting, boiling, baking, stewing, frying, steaming and heating: hot plates, hot closets, hot air and hot hearths with all manner of cocks for hot water and cold water and warm water and steam, and twenty saucepans all ticketed and labelled placed up to their necks in a vapour bath.'

In the kitchen a menu for a dinner served in January 1817 lists thirty-six entrées; several dishes were served in each course and guests helped themselves. The 'entrées volantes' ('flying dishes') were served usually with or after the fish. At a dinner given by Queen Victoria in about 1840 there were seventy dishes. The first course included 'four soups, four fish, four hors d'oeuvres, four relevés, sixteen entrées and three joints on the sideboard including a haunch of venison; the second course 'six roasts, six relevés, two flancs, four contre-flancs and sixteen entremets'. 'Flancs' were side-dishes which 'flanked' main dishes on the table or sideboard. 'Entremets' were also side-dishes and might consist of vegetables or sweets. The table was cleared after the sweets to make room for dessert and ices and an epergne, an elaborate ornament which held flowers or fruit.

It is often well worth visiting great houses open to the public many of which have kitchens worth a visit in themselves, and containing a wonderful range of utensils.

The kitchen at the Royal Pavilion, Brighton.

More lighting equipment

Simple lamps filled with animal or vegetable fat and a wick persisted well into the 19th century in rural parts of the United States. These were often called 'betty' or 'phoebe' lamps. Rushlights were also used; the pith of the soft rush was dipped repeatedly in melted fat and then put into an iron clamp and lit. Candles were made on a similar principle—a wick was surrounded with tallow, beeswax or some combustible vegetable substance. Candle boxes held the precious objects and were decorated by the Pennsylvania Dutch in bright colours with bold designs. Oil lamps were made by the bronze-casting firm of Fletcher and Gardiner which was renowned for the quality of its products until the end of the century. In 1787 John Miles of Birmingham in England patented the agitable burner, which used whale oil, and by 1830 the whale-oil lamp had become a standard fixture in the average American home. The glass industries of Cambridge, Sandwich and Pittsburgh made great quantities of these lamps, as did local pewterers and tinsmiths.

Though natural gas was first used by David Melville of Newport, Rhode Island, in 1806 it did not become popular until after the Civil War. Kerosene had replaced all other burning fluids by the end of the century. It became cheap when the oil fields of Pennsylvania were opened in about 1859. Kerosene lamps were made from glass, pottery, brass, bronze and a number of metal alloys. Art glass was also used. The best source for popular taste in lighting at the end of the 19th century is the Sears Roebuck Catalogue.

Matches were invented in the early part of the 19th century. Until then, fire-lighting was quite an art; coals from the previous night's fire or flint-wheel and tinder-box had to be used. Matches were kept in decorative little holders which hung on the wall. Made in tin, cast-iron and brass, they were advertised as 'Square Match Safes', 'Twin Match Safes', 'Match Box Holder and Safe'. A 'Match Scratcher' advertised in the early 20th century was made of tin and had a striking surface of best emery cloth.

Top: Candle mould. Left: match-holder and striker. Right: match-striker of wood and iron. All late 19th century.

Spits, ranges and cookers

The history of the cooker, from the medieval open fire in the centre of the room to today's electric stove, is fascinating. Until the invention of the enclosed kitchen range with a boxed-in oven in the early 19th century, all cooking was done over an open fire, at first in the centre of the room, then at the side. Meat was roasted on spits held by a pair of andirons. These wheelspits were turned by a rope running to a wooden pulley wheel driven by a clockwork mechanism known as a spit jack—which makes a very interesting and decorative collector's item. In the 16th and 17th centuries large stone fireplaces also had a fireback to protect the back brickwork and reflect the heat; these are often dated and are also collector's items. Simpler spits had cranked handles which were turned sometimes by a small boy, sometimes by a dog on a treadwheel and sometimes by a rope and series of pulley wheels.

The next major development was the large cast-iron cooking range with a central open fire flanked on one side by a roaster with movable shelves and on the other by a boiler with a brass tap for hot water. The top had a hot plate which would heat flat irons and boil saucepans when the detachable iron covers were removed. Some of these open ranges were still used for banquets in the 20th century. One example is now on display in the Science Museum, London.

Experiments in gas cooking were begun in the 1830s, but it was thought that impurities would affect the food. In 1837 James Sharp, who became engineer and manager of the Southampton Gas Company, demonstrated cooking by gas and in 1841 the great Alexis Soyer, head chef of the Reform Club in London, pioneered the use of gas. It was not until 1850 that gas cookers were offered for sale, however. They were heavy and usually made of sheet iron, sometimes consisting only of a hot plate, sometimes designed primarily for roasting.

Electric cookers were introduced in 1894, at the same time as electric lighting. At first they had unreliable heating elements and were slow and expensive to use. Oven thermostats were not introduced until 1923.

Cast-iron gas cooker, with no oven, by Alfred Kings of Liverpool, of an 1859 design, installed in the Rothschilds' house in Piccadilly, London. It had three circular burners controlled by three brass taps.

Tinware

Tinware was at first imported into America from England, but by the 1740s, the tinware firm of Edward and William Pattison had already begun operations at Berlin, Connecticut. Sheet tin was made into innumerable objects and was decorated with simple repousse work, scalloped edges, fancy punch-work and less frequently with attached ornaments. It was also painted and japanned. Women were extensively employed on painting and 'japanning' or lacquering—in fact one, Anna Maria Hayland, informed the public at Charlestown in 1751 that at the house of her late mother Elizabeth Sandwill 'she performed any kind of braziery and tinwork as her mother used to do'.

The range of kitchen tinware is very extensive, reflecting ever-increasing demand in the 18th century. The growth of the finished-metal trade was aided by increasing iron production. William Branson had a steel furnace in Philadelphia in 1730 and in 1762 Whitehead Humphrey started one too; in 1769 he went into partnership with John Zane and they took over the Trenton Steel Works. In 1768 Sharp and Curtenius had an ironworks in Manhattan and started casting 'stoves, plates, pots and kettles'. The American Revolution stopped production to some extent, but after the war Hartford County was dotted with new tin-making shops. So much tinware was then being produced that mechanics and peddlers were sent to Canada and the South, where they established agencies.

Styles of selling were often remarkable. Some journeymen or peddlers had a wagon fitted as a travelling shop, and there were 'floating tinshops' on rafts and barges on the Mississippi which made and repaired tinware. In the 1840s (the 'Fabulous Forties') the number of factories increased.

Cake-cutters, known in the trade as 'hearts, rounds, and diamonds' were one of the staple products of the tin manufacturers. Lists of tinware from contemporary mail-order catalogues include: 'tin coffee pots, tea pots, bread pans, pie plates, patty pans, dripping pans, box graters, biscuit cutters, basting spoons, tin cups, tin dipper, vegetable fork, and tin wash basins'. Among the New England families who worked in the tin trade were the Pattisons of Berlin, Connecticut, the Upsons of Marion, the Norths of Berlin, Manross of Bristol and William Miter. The Filley family of Bloomfield had a very complete collection of family papers which contain much information on the early manufacture of American tinware.

American graters of the turn of the 19th century—graters such as these came in sets with different-sized holes.

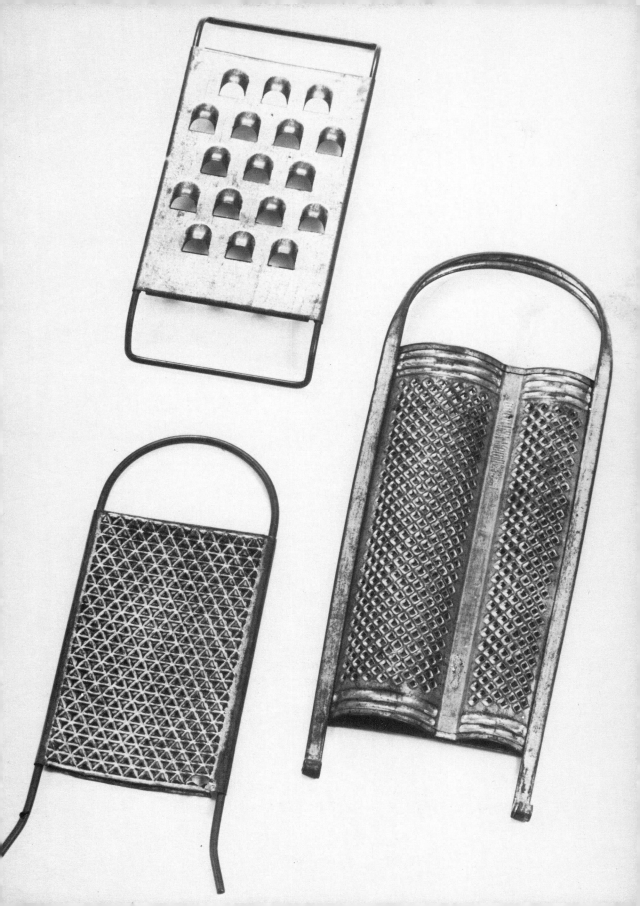

Baking utensils

Until the late 18th century very little tinware was used in America, but the demand increased in the first half of the 19th century; what was made became expensive and greatly prized. The local 'whitesmiths' (a name for tin-workers as opposed to iron-workers) attempted to meet this demand; they required a comparatively small amount of equipment: a special anvil called a 'stock' on which to turn the edges of the tin before soldering them together; a small furnace with a charcoal fire in which to heat the soldering iron; the solder itself (a composition of tin and lead); some tools shaped for special purposes; and hammers and mallets. After making a pattern, the whitesmith would mark it out on the sheet of tin-plate and cut it out with shears. Any ornamentation was put on before the sections were soldered.

American housewives in the 18th century had to be self-sufficient and prided themselves on their 'baking' talents. For one Thanksgiving dinner in New England in 1779 'all the baking of pies and cakes was done at our house and we had the big oven heated and filled twice each day for three days before it was all done', so a letter-writer recounted. Another writer in New England in the 1830s related that there was no baker in his grandfather's village: 'each family bakes its own bread, cake and pies'.

Pies and puddings were the usual dessert course in England and America. A form of self-raising flour was introduced in the 1840s but it did not catch on until about 1870. Baking powder was used instead; it could be made at home but was also manufactured and sold in packets. A wide range of pie tins can be collected, including shallow and deep pie plates, jelly cake pans, loose-bottom pie plates, etc.

Pastry knives, crimpers or jaggers have been in common use since the 17th century. The first ones had an open-spoked wheel, and the handles were either chamfered or flattened into a curved blade. Eighteenth-century examples had solid wheels with a shaped cutter at the end of the handle for ornamenting; these were made of cast-brass and also of wrought-iron. These are very interesting items to collect, for they are also made in steel, wood, ivory. Some American 'scrimshaw' examples were made from whale ivory—the New Bedford Whaling Museum, New Bedford, Massachusetts, has some fine examples.

Pie tin, c. 1850; pie-tin remover, 1900; pastry-crimper, c. 1860.

Cookie-cutters and muffin pans

Pennsylvania Dutch and German housewives traditionally made at least a bushel of cookies in decorative shapes for Christmas. Early cutters were quite large and came in a variety of shapes—horses, doves, cockerels, people and the American eagle are just a few examples. Another figure was 'Belznickel', the symbol of Christmas among the Pennsylvania Germans until the mid-19th century (Santa Claus is a comparatively late innovation!). He brought cookies, candies and toys to children and would go from house to house dressed in old clothes and carrying a stick in one hand. Reindeer, mounted figures and clowns were other attractive shapes—those especially interested should visit the collections in the Philadelphia Museum of Art and Landis Valley Museum, Landis Valley, Pennsylvania.

To the New World the Germans brought their traditional Christmas honey cakes, marzipan and gingerbread. The moulds for imposing patterns on the cake dough or almond paste were called 'Springerle' or marzipan moulds. Tin cutters were cheaper and quicker to make, but the hand-carved moulds had been minor masterpieces. Rural tinsmiths made these cutters before they were mass-produced. The shapes were very varied—horses, deer, birds, stars and hearts. In 1902 they were even on sale advertising 'Card Party Cake Cutters' for cakes resembling the different denominations of cards. For collecting, look for unusual shapes and details; stars and crescents as well as animals and people are quite common.

Muffins were often served for breakfast. The dough (made of flour or sometimes of potatoes and flour) was made in the evening, put to rise all night in the warm and baked in muffin rings, pans or on a griddle. A cookery book published in Vermont in 1845 describes the rough-and-ready method of testing the heat of the oven before the invention of the thermostat: 'For pies, cakes and white bread the heat of the oven should be such that you can hold your hand and arm in while you count 40. For brown bread, meats, beans, Indian puddings and pumpkin pies it should be hotter so that you can only hold it in while you count 20.'

Similar items collectors should look out for are cookie tins, in which the biscuits were kept after they had been made. The Pennsylvania Dutch painted these with brightly-coloured flowers and other motifs.

Cookie-cutter, c. 1880; muffin pan, early 20th century.

Rolling-pins

Ordinary wooden rolling-pins have changed little in shape over a long period of time. An early 17th-century illustration of a bakery shows a pastrycook rolling out dough with a rolling-pin similar to the one illustrated opposite. In New England men and boys spent the long winter evenings making numerous small objects such as trenchers, spoons and churns—a profitable use of spare time. As the demand grew, so such objects were mass-produced in factories. In 1902 Sears Roebuck advertised rolling-pins with revolving handles for only six cents. Another type had carved designs; these were known as biscuit- and cake-rollers and saved time and trouble—they were rolled across the dough which took an impression of their pattern and then the whole piece of dough was transferred on a tin plate to the oven. The biscuits were cut out with a sharp knife when cooked. Convex rolling pins in various hardwoods were used for making pie-crusts, thin in the middle and thicker round the edges. Another roller with sharp indentations was used for crushing oatmeal and salt.

Another type of roller was used not for cooking but for pressing hand-made lace. A piece of flannel was wrapped round the roller; then the carefully washed lace was rolled around it and left to dry. Once the lace was dry the roller was turned a few times and it was slipped off, flat and undamaged.

Porcelain rolling-pins could be filled with water to give added weight and also to keep the pastry cool. They were more easily cleaned than wooden ones—a sign that people were becoming more hygiene-conscious. Porcelain pins sometimes had advertisements for flour printed on them.

Rolling-pins were often given as wedding gifts in a set with a potato-masher.

A lithograph by L. Prang of 1874 depicts a 'modernized' kitchen but the lady rolling pastry on a table is using the kind of rolling-pin which had been used long before and is still in use today.

Rolling-pins: left, wood, c. 1800; centre, wood, 1840; right, porcelain, early 20th century.

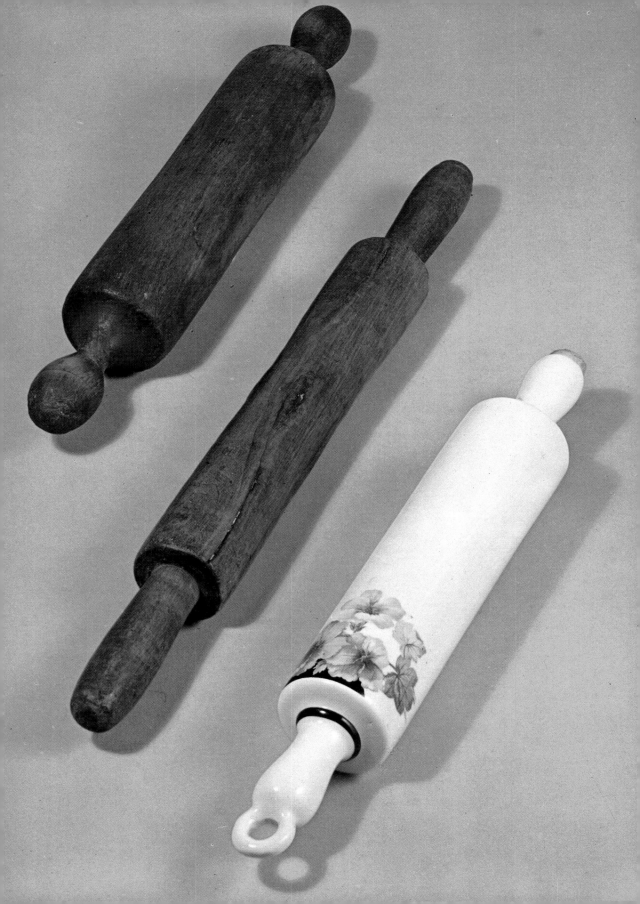

Gingerbread and biscuit moulds

From Tudor and later household recipes we know that decorating food is a very old custom. Gingerbread was decorated by pressing the spiced dough into wooden moulds. On special occasions the gingerbreads were gilded and given as presents. They were popular items at fairs and the gingerbread stall was one of the last to survive at St Bartholomew's Fair, held annually at Smithfield in London from 1123 until 1850.

Moulds, or 'cards' as they were sometimes called, were often carved on both sides and were made from boxwood, beach, walnut and pearwood. Among the many subjects available were Punch (a favourite at fairs for centuries), Moses and Aaron, Adam and Eve, the Crucifixion, St Catherine, Queen Elizabeth and the Duke of Wellington.

Collectors are most likely to come across moulds from the 19th or late 18th centuries. In the 19th century several carvers specialized in food moulds and stamped them with their name. Among them are William Henry Mathews of 22 Lant Street, Borough in South London, who was in business between 1839 and 1851 and whose trade was continued by Alfred Mathews until about 1878, and William Hawkins of 4 Vigo Street, Piccadilly, who made high-grade moulds between 1838 and 1851.

Wooden moulds were not only made for pastrycooks but also for other decorators, plasterers for instance. Pastrycooks' moulds are never backed, nor are they painted on the end grain. They are between $\frac{1}{2}$ and $1\frac{1}{4}$ inches thick, although there are exceptions. Unless made of boxwood, they tend to be worn and rounded on both sides.

Collectors should look for quality of carving and of type of wood used and for interesting and rare subjects and designs. Beware of decorators' moulds which have been altered to look like food moulds by having their backing removed and screw-holes filled in. Wooden fakes are nearly all crudely carved, for they are produced as cheaply as possible; the most usual motifs are cats, dogs and other undatable subjects.

Top: rectangular wooden mould dating from reign of William IV. Bottom, left to right: mould with alphabet motifs; rectangular stoneware mould; rolling-pin marked with Queen Victoria's initials. All these are of the late 18th and 19th centuries. In the background is a baker's poster of the period.

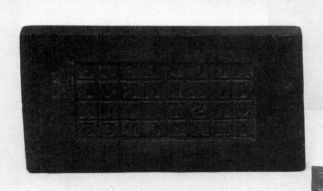

Glass rolling-pins

Glass rolling-pins, often known as 'love tokens', were made at glassworks near English ports—Bristol, London, Sunderland and Newcastle, for instance. They were frequently decorated with ships, departing sailors and inscriptions such as 'be true to me', 'for my mother' and 'may the eye of the Lord watch over you'. Many held salt and were hung by the side of the fire to keep the salt dry. Salt taxes rose steadily after 1694 until repealed in 1845 and made salt very expensive, so these salt-filled rolling-pins were a two-in-one present.

The term 'Nailsea glass' describes a style of glass decorated with festooning, mottling and flecking: hot molten glass was rolled in coloured and/or white enamel chips which were sprinkled on the marver plate. The mass of glass was reheated and finally blown into the required form, the colours being incorporated in the glass. Because of the high tax on flint glass, 'bottle glass' was cheaper, since it was taxed at one-fifth the rate. Bottle glass was rather drab and so the splashes of colour described helped to brighten it up. Much glass attributed to the Nailsea works, which functioned between 1788 and 1873, was in fact made elsewhere, in Bristol, Stourbridge, Newcastle, Yorkshire, Wrockwardine in Shropshire, Warrington, St Helens and Alloa in Scotland.

Other methods of decoration used were painting, gilding and printing. Rolling-pins were advertised with sea-faring motifs: thus, 'Sailor's charm. Glass rolling-pins for hanging in a Ship's Cabin, white decorated in colours, with ships, motto and inscription.'

Rolling-pins with attractive transfer designs and inscriptions are much sought after, and reproductions of the early decorated types have been made in great numbers since 1910. They continue to appear in so-called 'Bristol blue', lavishly gilded with nautical and domestic decorations.

Seven rolling-pins made of Nailsea glass; 19th century.

Slipware baking dishes

The two dishes illustrated opposite are representative of some of the most charmingly naive and long-lived types of English pottery, called 'slipware' because they are decorated in 'slip'—a clay diluted with water to a creamy consistency and 'trailed' onto an object as decoration. Sometimes the clay was diluted further and used as an overall dip. Such ware (including dishes, mugs and jugs) was made at many country potteries all over Europe, England and America. Early examples have 'toothed' or notched rims, later rims are plain. Very decorative slipware dishes were made in the 17th century by potters such as Ralph and Thomas Toft and Ralph Simpson; these are rare and costly collector's items, as are the wares of the Kentish pottery at Wrotham.

Some slipware dishes were made as gifts or decorative objects, others had practical uses, as baking dishes for instance. One traditional style was 'combed' ware. Formed of low-quality inexpensive clay, the dish was coated with a thin slip of whitish refined clay to cover the rough body; then the design was trailed on in different coloured slips with a simple slip-jug or slip-trailer. The combed effect was produced by drawing a bristle or similar thin object across the lines.

In America such trailed slipware was made in Pennsylvania and North Carolina in particular and in Tennessee. The Pennsylvania Dutch community produced some remarkable (and now very rare) sgraffito pie plates, with the decoration being scratched through the glaze to the clay beneath.

Apart from the more obviously decorative wares like Bennington and Rockingham, American 'useful' pottery is still almost untouched by collectors, and baking dishes were made in red, yellow, and white clays glazed and unglazed. The collector should look at and, if possible, handle as many examples as he can so as to familiarize himself with the style and 'feel' of the dishes.

Two slipware baking dishes made in Derbyshire, the oval one in 1787, the rectangular one 1860.

Cauldrons and pressure-cookers

From the Bronze Age until the 19th century the cauldron was an essential cooking utensil and was used in a variety of ways. The earliest cauldrons were of bronze, hammered iron and copper. In the 19th century they were made of cast-iron and cast in two halves upside down over a clay core; the vertical casting seams can still be seen. Some were made with three feet (this was a shape known even in ancient Chinese bronzes) to enable them to stand in the fire itself; others had a rounded base and a swing handle from which they were suspended by a chain and hook or from a chimney crane. Cauldrons were used to heat water, boil meat and cook stews and also for baking bread.

Some 18th- and 19th-century manufacturers of saucepans and skillets, as the long-handled pans were called, were Thomas Palmer, Wasborough, Warner and Kenrick; their names are sometimes found on handles. The skillet evolved from the cauldron but was used concurrently. The first skillets also had three feet and long handles so that the cook did not have to get too close to the fire. Other pans in use were copper saucepans with tinned interiors, frying pans or 'spiders', made in both iron and copper. In addition there were specially shaped utensils for specific foods: ham-kettles, which were large-lidded pans shaped like a ham; long, narrow fish-kettles with an inner pierced drainer; turbot-kettles also shaped like fish; and steamers and bain-maries, which held a number of saucepans over boiling water.

Pressure-cookers were thought of as early as 1680, when Denis Papin F.R.S. exhibited to the Royal Society his 'New Digester or Engine for softening bones'. It had a pressure of 35 to 50 pounds per square inch and was a dangerous piece of equipment—modern examples have a maximum of 15 pounds. The 19th-century digester was the forerunner of the modern pressure-cooker. A conical weight fitted inside the lid was raised for steam to escape when pressure exceeded two or three pounds per square inch.

Above: two 19th-century cast-iron cauldrons. Below: a pair of 19th-century pressure-cookers.

Saucepans

Iron and copper were used in the manufacture of the first cooking pots, but were soon replaced first by tin and enamel and later by aluminium and steel. In Victorian times copper was confined to the richer households, but even so a wide variety of pans was made in copper: saucepans also known as skillets, fish kettles and turbot pans, stock pots (which sometimes had a tap at the base for drawing off the liquid), kettles, frying pans, sauté pans, cutlet pans, omelette pans, bain-maries, baking sheets and all kinds of moulds. So the collector has a wide choice. Copper utensils were taken to a local smith for repair. On the inside they were cleaned with sand; in 1893 Mrs Kellogg, in her book *Science in the Kitchen* advised that 'copper utensils may be brightened by the use of vinegar and salt, or oxalic acid.'

While Great Britain fostered the production of raw materials in the colonies, she intended to manufacture all the goods they required herself. The American colonists, however, soon objected to the profits England was making out of them and started to make what they needed themselves. Copper was first mined, at Cranby in Connecticut, in the early 18th century; extensive deposits of metallic copper were found in the Lake Superior district and copper mines were established at Cornwall, Connecticut, and Bucks County, Pennsylvania. By the turn of the 19th century the American housewife was being offered pans in imperial hollow stoveware, which was a smooth cast grey iron, in cast aluminium ware, solid steel lava-enamelled ware, peerless enamelled ware and true blue enamelled ware—and all this in a bewildering variety of shapes and sizes.

The collector should easily be able to build up a wide-ranging selection of 19th-century stoveware. Most important of all is to get to know the look and the 'feel' of old metal, for there are many modern reproductions.

Copper saucepan and iron pot-hanger; both 19th century.

Pot hooks and cranes

Cranes were hinged horizontal bars onto which were forged hanging pieces with a hook; they held utensils over the fire and were screwed onto the beams at the side of the fireplace or bricked into the wall itself. They were needed to hold heavy weights and enabled kettles and large saucepans to be swung backwards and forwards over the heat. Another means of roasting joints before an open fire was the bottle-jack, which could also be hooked onto a chimney crane. These were made of brass or japanned metal and sometimes had their maker's mark on a decorative plaque—Linwood is one of the most famous manufacturers. The jacks contained a clockwork mechanism and the joints suspended from the hook below the jack rotated above a dripping-pan. *The Ironmongers Trade Journal* for 1860 carried an advertisement from F. W. Gerish of East Road, City Road, London, for 'Every description of Ornamental Gate or other Fancy Hinges—Gothic, Medieval and Elizabethan or made to any Design'. The advertisement continued: 'Oven Doors. Sets of Ironwork for Ovens, Register Stoves, Ranges, etc.'

Cranes first appeared in the 17th century but continued in use until the late 19th century—and no doubt remained in some rural cottages well into the 20th century. Many cranes were made by the local blacksmith. The blacksmith's ledgers of the Hedges family list pot hooks, gridirons and spits. Bottle-jacks, both japanned and of brass, were still advertised in Harrod's catalogue of 1895. Pot hooks could be used in a number of ways: hooked onto a chimney crane, fitted on an iron bar with links of chain to adjust the height, hooked on two sliding bars punched with a series of holes (an iron pin could be used to adjust the height), and on a ratchet, that is, a flat bar with teeth.

At the Museum of Rural Life in Reading a fine wrought-iron crane is displayed; it has a large hook which holds a big kettle with a tilting handle—thus one could pour from the kettle without removing it from the hook.

A writer describes the kitchen in his grandfather's home in New England in the 1830s: 'Of course there was a crane to hang kettles on. The brass kettles, of various sizes, were kind of dress-up kettles; the iron kettles were the everyday ones. They had legs so they would either sit on the hearth next to the fire, or hang by a pot hook on the crane.'

Two very attractive 19th-century brass cranes, and four pot-hooks—the one ornamented with two small kettles is particularly pleasing.

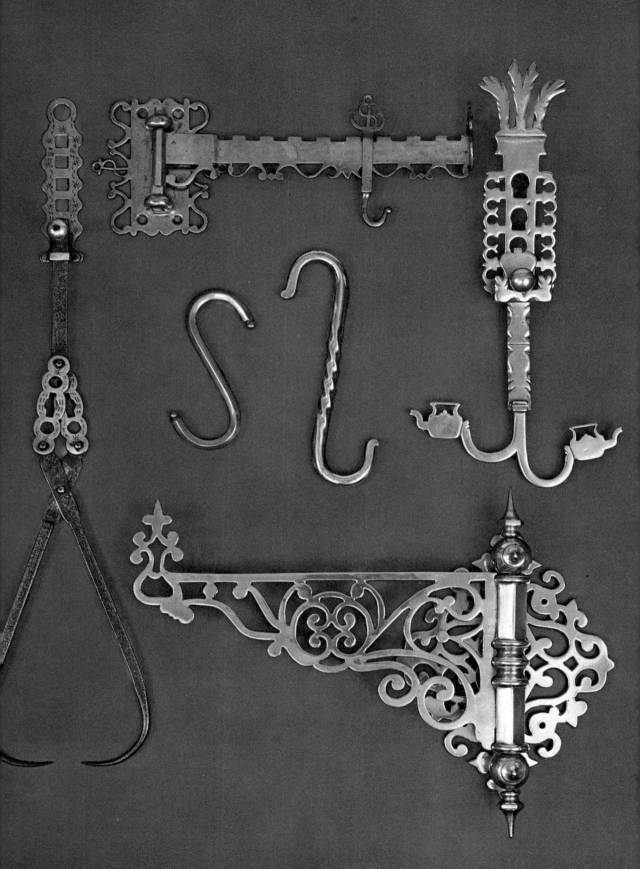

Tureens and jelly moulds

Tureens like the one shown were first made by Wedgwood in 1790. Early ones had a removable inner lining in which meats used in pies or pâtés were cooked before being served at table in the decorative outer case. Both the sides and the lids of some tureens were moulded with vegetables, game birds, hares and pigeons; others were decorated with fine lattice-work to simulate pastry. During the late 18th century and the early years of the 19th, when flour was scarce because of bad harvests, these dishes were used instead of real pie-crust. In Captain Jeffs' book, *The Life of George (Beau) Brummell* (1844), he says: 'The scarcity two years after Brummell's retirement [1800] was so great that the consumption of flour for pastry was prohibited in the Royal Household, rice being used instead. The distillers left off malting, hackney coach fares were raised 25 per cent and Wedgwood made dishes to represent pie-crust.' Later tureens had a glazed interior surface and no lining.

Wedgwood also made jelly-moulds. The moulds illustrated opposite are unusual in that they are in two parts: the jelly was put in the outer container and the inner 'shape' inserted. When the jelly was set and turned out, the inner mould acted as a support and its attractive design was visible through the jelly. Such moulds were also made by other potters, among them Wilson and Neale. Unfortunately it is rare to find these double moulds complete. Wedgwood also made plain creamware moulds with moulded designs; cheaper models were made in brown salt-glaze.

Jellies were the prerogative of the rich in the 18th century and in the early part of the 19th century as well. The Great Exhibition of 1851 popularized them, though table jellies in packets were not extensively used before 1880.

When buying pottery and porcelain, remember that the condition of the object will influence its price to a considerable extent. Items should be examined carefully for chips and cracks and especially for repairs, which are very skilful these days.

Above: Wedgwood game-pie tureen of a type first made in 1790, and continued throughout the 19th century. Below: three Wedgwood jelly moulds of the 1780s—an obelisk, a pyramid, and a wedge shape with its outer cover.

Decorative tureens

Fish dishes were designed to hold a fish mousse or perhaps 'potted lobsters'. In *Modern Cookery* (1845) Eliza Acton gives a recipe for the mousse and instructs that after the mixture has been pressed into a potting pan or mould it should be sent to table 'neatly garnished with light green foliage or with ornamentally cut paper fastened round the mould'.

A number of factories made decorative tureens. Mintons and George Jones manufactured game and pie tureens, moulded in relief with game birds, rabbits, hares and pigeons. These appear in their range of popular so-called 'majolica' ware, which imitated Italian lead-glazed pottery.

Of course many other pottery dishes and jars were used in the kitchen. Eliza Acton illustrates a Nottingham jar and cover, a brown stoneware jar of a shape still made today. Nottingham stoneware is a distinctively English type of pottery—made from the beginning of the 18th century until the 1790s. Similar wares were made in Staffordshire and at Belper, near Derby, Brampton, Chesterfield, and at Codnor Park and Denby, where excellent stoneware is produced to this day.

Moulded dishes and tureens were also made in America. Some have been attributed to potteries in Milwaukee, but moulded and decorated stonewares, usually with a dark blue slip glaze were made in Illinois, Pennsylvania and Ohio. Simpler stonewares, often with blue or salt-glazed decoration, were made in many potteries, particularly in the East and Midwest.

The various types of stoneware would make a most interesting collection and could be displayed with an illustration from a contemporary advertisement or cookery book. Watch out for possible repairs when looking for items.

Staffordshire pottery dish moulded as a fish, the knop formed as a lobster which is gilded—the dish contains an inner liner; 19th century.

Copper moulds

Copper jelly-moulds are among the most attractive items of kitchen-ware. The range of shapes and sizes is virtually unlimited; as part of the *batterie de cuisine* of great houses, the moulds often bore the name of the house or their owner's initials. There are over five hundred moulds marked DWL (Duke of Wellington, London), in the Royal Pavilion Kitchen in Brighton.

Moulds were made of copper and tinned on the interior. Elaborately-shaped examples were used for recipes such as Constantia Jelly, so called from the Constantia wine (a sweet wine from South Africa) used in the recipe, 'blanc-mange' or 'blanc-manger' and 'jaune-manger', sometimes called 'Dutch flummery'. Moulds for savoury and vegetable entrées were advertised under the names of Crawfish, King Fisher, Hare, Fancy Cutlet, Ham, Bird's Nest, Ox Tongue, Chicken. Round 'Timbale' moulds were used for moulding rice and savoury timbales. Harrod's Trade Catalogue of 1895 (available in reference libraries) illustrates and prices thirty-nine different shapes of copper moulds—and each shape came in a number of sizes! It would be interesting to try to collect every shape illustrated in the Harrod's Catalogue—though I fear the prices will be very different today! An oval mould with fluted sides and a recumbent lion on the top cost 1s. 6d. for the 1½-pint size, and an elaborate oval copper jelly-mould in the 1¾-pint size cost 10s. 9d. Some moulds are specified as being either for jelly or for cake, and some have covers (viz. a 'round melon mould'). There were also raised pie moulds with clips at the side which released the moulds from the pastry pie. One of these is illustrated in Eliza Acton's *Modern Cookery* of 1845, and a similar example is shown in the Harrod's Catalogue fifty years later.

Collectors should beware modern copies of copper utensils, though a careful study of genuine old moulds will enable the collector to spot copies. Utensils occasionally come on the market at auctions in old houses: included in a sale at Cullen House in Scotland in autumn 1975 were two *batteries de cuisine*, each of thirty or forty copper saucepans with lids and all marked with the name of the house.

Copper moulds of the 19th and early 20th centuries; a 'castle' mould, top right; a plain, ring or 'timbale' mould; and a set of four moulds of succeeding sizes.

Butter, candy and ice moulds

Butter moulds were used from quite early times to put designs on butter. In England they were mostly carved in sycamore, the best quality ones in boxwood. The motifs sometimes gave clues about the type of farm from which the butter came: a swan meant a river farm, a sheep a hill farm. Rare designs include one for Easter, a cross and two eggs, and one for Queen Victoria's Jubilee. It is thought that Swiss settlers introduced the butter mould to America. To produce 'print' butter (as opposed to butter packed in crocks and tubs) was laborious but worth time and effort, as it fetched more money at market. Popular American designs include tulips, thistles, wheatsheaves, hearts. Some have initials and dates and others were used for advertising: 'Good Butter—Taste It'. In the 19th century the manufacture of butter moulds became a minor trade; they were turned on a lathe and then carved by hand. Do not confuse these moulds with bag-stamps, used for printing homespun bags for taking grain to the mill.

In the harsh Victorian age, when children were meant to be seen and not heard, children probably only had candy or 'sweets' on special occasions. They were very probably home made. Moulds for making a cone of maple sugar were manufactured in wood in two halves which were held together by bands. Mrs Marshall's School of Cookery in London advertised tin moulds for making chocolates, fondants etc. at 1s.6d. per dozen.

Ice cream was first made in the 18th century but became more generally popular during the 19th. Ice cream moulds were made in a variety of shapes in pewter and copper. They sometimes had detachable lids and bases which made the ices easy to remove. The cream was poured into the moulds which were then put into an ice-cave or ice-chest; these had been developed from ice-houses on country estates. Some pewter moulds came as a set—the inner holding the cream, the outer larger one shaved ice. By 1902 Sears Roebuck were advertising bucket-type ice-cream freezers and also a number of refrigerators, including models for large and small apartment houses.

Left above: iron ice mould; early 20th century. Right: copper fish-shaped candy mould; 1880. Below: wooden butter mould, c. 1750.

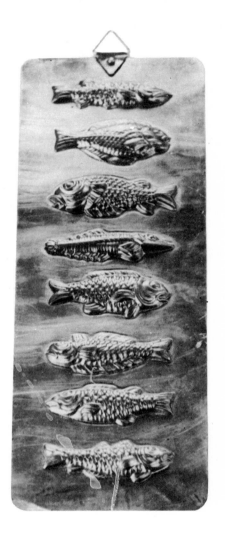

More moulds

Copper is one of the oldest metals known to man. Early in the 19th century, vessels were made of spun copper, which is sheet-thin and malleable enough to spin on a lathe. The corn mould reminds us that Indian corn was a staple grain in every colony—it had been cultivated by the Indians and there were a great number of varieties. 'Corn shuckings' were great social gatherings; in November, when some of the more pressing farm jobs had been finished, a great pile of unshucked corn was stacked on the ground and a large bonfire was lit at a safe distance. If a man found a red ear of corn he had the right to kiss the girl of his choice—if he could catch her. Thus corn was the symbol of neighbourliness and also an important crop and animal feed. The pineapple was a symbol of welcome, and as such an appropriate motif to have on jellies and creams to be served to guests; so moulds with pineapple designs were often made.

Cheaper moulds were made in tin, pewter, glass and earthenware; these had less elaborate designs. Some moulds for cakes had supporting feet; moulds with lids were used for steaming puddings. The melon-shaped mould was a favourite with the Pennsylvania Dutch. Towards the end of the 19th century, moulds were used as advertising aids—Brown & Polson in England, who made cornflour for blancmange, produced earthenware moulds with printed recipes, and in America the famous Jell-O firm gave away metal moulds with the name of the firm stamped on the base. From the 1760s on, copper moulds were almost always lined with tin, since it had been discovered that un-tinned copper was the source of much illness. American-made copper moulds before the middle of the 19th century are rare and were almost always hand made.

In building a collection, look for the huge variety of design and the sharpness of the detail. Simple rounded shapes, while pleasant in themselves, are found in great numbers, as they were easy to mass-produce. Figures, special symbols, castles, all these are greatly prized and worth looking for. To appreciate the difference between a modern, cheaply-made copy and a Victorian or turn-of-the-century mould, make up a gelatine dessert; when it is set, turn out both moulds. The first will be fairly simple, the edges rounded everywhere so that the design is shallow and doesn't stand out, the old mould will give intricate detail and crisp outline, and show what to look for.

Above: tin fish-shaped mould; c. 1850. Below left: copper 'corn' mould; c. 1880. Right: copper 'pineapple' mould; 1900.

Simple utensils

All the utensils shown opposite have been in use for hundreds of years and can still be found in modern kitchens, though of course the metals from which they are made have changed slightly! Cooking forks were derived from the Roman 'flesh hook' and were essential when cooking meat on spits in front of an open fire. The large, shallow, perforated skimming spoons (sometimes called 'fleeters') were used for taking scum and fat off the top of large pans of boiling food and preserves. In the dairy they were also used to take the cream off the top of the milk to be made into butter. At the turn of the 19th century the Sears Roebuck catalogue (known sometimes in rural areas as *The Wish Book*) listed a 'Housekeeper's Outfit of Tinware' for the bargain price of one dollar thirty cents; it included such things as a 'wood handled slotted mixing spoon' and a 'tinned steel Kitchen Fork with three prongs'. Ladles and spoons were also made of wood and were sometimes decorated with carved patterns, initials and dates.

Tin came into vogue in America after the War of Independence, and peddlers travelled around the country with their wares. The housewife liked tin for its lightness and shining surface. The collector should be able to find a wide range of these smaller 'hardware' items, both of wood and metal.

Left to right: Tin spatula, c. 1890; iron skimmer, late 19th century; tin spatula, c. 1910; iron cooking fork, 1870.

Choppers

Choppers have been in use in kitchens all over the world for a very long time—indeed the chopper ranks as one of the most essential implements. Choppers with rounded blades were often used in their own chopping bowl, the well of which was hollowed out to fit the blade of the chopper. Initially made by local smiths, they soon became a factory product. As late as 1902, however, Sears Roebuck were still advertising specialized choppers such as 'slaw cutters' and a potato and vegetable cutter described as 'a household convenience for making Saratoga chips, cutting slaw or slicing fruits and vegetables'. It is interesting to note that the advertisement stresses 'convenience'—something that was to be demanded more and more as the 20th century progressed.

To meet this demand, the first food-chopping machine was invented in the late 19th century. Two examples of these are the 'Eclipse Solid Steel Mincer—handle and blade formed of one piece of bright steel' and the 'Gem Solid Steel Mincer'; in 1902 the former retailed for eight cents and the latter for twenty-seven cents. Choppers were also sold in conjunction with their chopping bowls and trays, both circular and oblong. Some Scandinavian choppers were heart-shaped, and this was a favourite design. One chopper, which required two hands, was made of three parallel iron blades which curved upwards at the ends and had a knob handle at each end. An 18th-century herb chopper had a cast-iron cutting-wheel on a double-ended wooden handle; the wheel was rolled backwards and forwards. Mincing-machines, which could be clamped onto the edge of the table, were in manufacture by the end of the 19th century and were known as 'meat choppers' in American mail-order catalogues.

Top to bottom: iron double-bladed chopper, early 20th century; small iron chopper, mid-19th century; rounded-blade chopper, c. 1860.

Apple-corers, sugar-nippers and skewers

Apple-corers and scoops have a very long history and Roman examples have even been found. Initially intended to help those without teeth to eat raw apples, they were later made for use as corers. They were also used for cheese and were sometimes known as 'cheese-spitters'. Made in a variety of materials—boxwood, sycamore, lignum vitae, ivory and silver—they present an interesting challenge to collectors to find examples in as many different materials as possible. Some dated scoops can be found (usually from the 18th and 19th centuries). Scoops carved with initials and given as love-tokens have hearts and other amatory motifs.

Sugar was a great luxury until trade with the West Indies developed in the 18th century. Sugar was bought by the grocers in great cone-shaped loaves. Nippers were used to break off pieces. The cones were about three feet high and weighed about fourteen pounds. The rich would buy a whole 'loaf', the poor only a few ounces cut off the loaf by the grocers. Nippers work on the principle of pliers—the jaws are almost circular and have a sharp blade at the end of each jaw. They were made in iron and steel and some late 18th-century examples have incised ornament on the flat surfaces. They were mostly for use in kitchen and shop, although some smaller models were made for the dining-room. Some sweet-manufacturers issued nippers to their clients, and some were still in use in sweet shops in the early part of this century.

Great joints of meat roasted on spits needed very sturdy skewers. These were made of steel with a loop handle at one end and hung from a special skewer hook. Beechwood skewers were also made.

Left top: two apple-corers made from sheep's bone; centre, two 18th-century pairs of sugar-cutters; right, a generously proportioned 18th-century meat skewer.

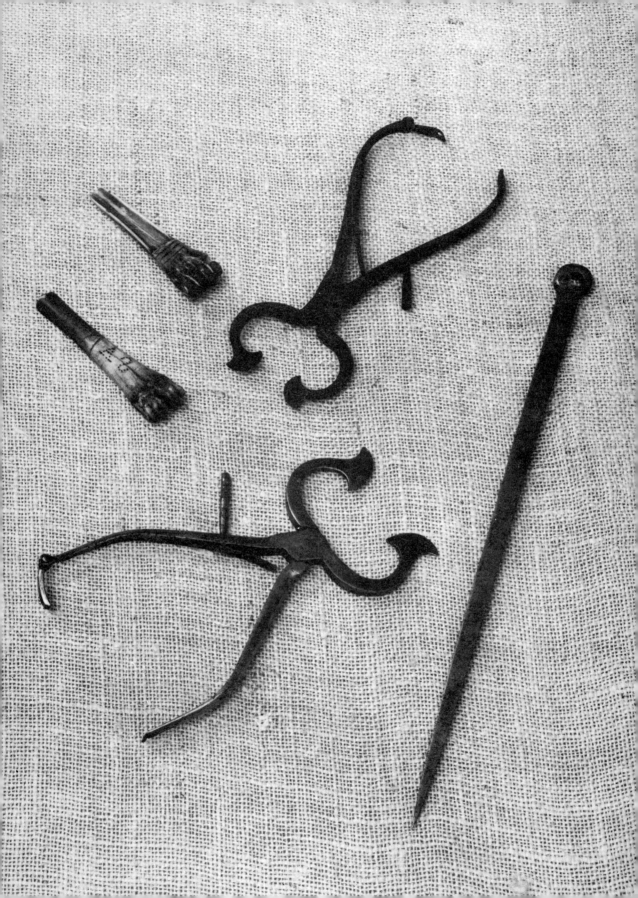

Mortars and pestles

A mortar is a vessel of hard material (ranging from wood to marble, brass, bronze and hard stoneware) with a cup-shaped cavity in which ingredients used in cooking and pharmacy are pounded with a pestle. From early times the mortar was the symbol of an apothecary. They were commonly used in Persia and Arab countries, where medicine was advanced in early times. In the Middle Ages a mortar was part of a set of cast-metal kitchen utensils given as a wedding present by rich parents to a daughter-in-law.

Mortars vary considerably in size, from floor-standing models to a mere 3 to 4 inches high. The former usually had a stone or marble bowl; the pestle for such mortars occasionally had a ring screwed in its top so that it could be suspended by a cord from a ceiling pulley and counterbalanced by a lead weight. A fine example of this type can be seen in the Great Kitchen of the Royal Pavilion, Brighton. The smaller mortars have a wide variety of external shapes—cylindrical, bell, hexagonal and octagonal, funnel and bowl. The wooden ones were made in oak, elm, beech, walnut and laburnum, though lignum vitae was probably the favourite, because of its hardness, impermeability and its imagined medicinal qualities. Wedgwood made mortars, often with a lip, in a hard white stoneware; the matching pestle had a wooden handle. It is hard for modern housewives, many of whom take for granted electric grinders, mincing-machines and liquidizers, to imagine the number of uses our ancestors found for a mortar and pestle: pounding herbs and spices, pulverizing coffee beans before coffee mills were invented, crushing salt, finely pounding sugar, which was first of all cut from the 'loaf', mashing vegetables and pounding meat.

Mortars were also used by apothecaries and in tobacco shops, inns and coffee houses to crush tobacco leaves into snuff. A flat-ended mortar and pestle called a 'washing dolly' was used for mangling lace.

Mortars are fascinating subjects for the collector, for basic shapes date back to the 17th century and decoration is very varied. Some of the wooden ones are outstanding examples of the turner's skill.

American-made mortars include wooden examples, as well as some in Parian ware from Vermont, and ironstone made in West Virginia and elsewhere. American ironstone which dates from about 1870 onwards, is still an undeveloped field for the collector—although some was poor and heavy, a number of factories made individual products as fine as any European factory.

Wooden mortar and pestle; mid-19th century.

Graters and grinders

The first coffee-houses were opened in London in 1652 by a Turkish merchant and became immediately popular as literary, artistic and commercial meeting-places. One of the first manufacturers of coffee-grinders was one Nicholas Brook, who lived 'at the sign of the Frying Pan, in St Tulie's Street against the Church'; he sold mills for forty to forty-five shillings—a high price, but they were finely turned in costly lignum vitae and the grinding cogs were of hand-forged steel. The collector who finds one of these mills is very fortunate. Coffee-grinders were frequently illustrated on grocers' trade cards in the second half of the 18th century.

Eighteenth-century mills were elegantly shaped, often in the form of classical urns, and were upright with screw-on tops; the handles were jointed and kept in the top chamber. In the later part of the century the screw-on top was replaced by a saucer-like receiver for the beans. The central spindle for the grinder had a folding detachable handle, kept in the lower compartment; today these are often missing. In the 19th century the handle became bigger and more secure; the receiving saucer was made of metal and the base had a drawer.

Spices have been used extensively in England since Norman times, both to preserve food and to enhance its taste. By the mid-17th century the Dutch had the monopoly of almost all trade in cloves, nutmegs, mace and cinnamon. It was only broken as spice plants spread through the colonies and their market value fell.

Nutmegs originated in the Moluccan islands which the Dutch conquered in 1667. In 1769 the French introduced nutmeg trees into Mauritius and by the end of the century the East India Company had established nutmeg trees in Penang, Malaya.

In the 18th century, nutmeg-graters were kept in decorative boxes of silver and enamel and carried about in the pocket, so that one could add nutmeg to mulled wine. Until the end of the 19th century the general-purpose kitchen grater consisted of a sheet of punched blued-iron screwed to a wooden backplate.

Top: English coffee-grinder by Archibald Kenrick; mid-19th century. Below: nutmeg grater in japanned tin plate with closed box for nutmeg; mid-19th century.

Spice cupboards and graters

Spices, which were expensive, were kept in cupboards which looked like miniature chests-of-drawers, complete with a key for the outer door. These early wooden boxes are beautiful examples of the turner's and carver's art. Some 17th-century examples were made as radiating divisioned boxes; screw-on lids kept them as airtight as possible. This type of box, which sometimes had a grater in the centre compartment, was the direct ancestor of the Victorian iron and japanned tin box. These were illustrated in Harrod's Catalogue of 1895; round ones ranged in price from 2s. 3d. to 3s. 5d. and square ones looked like cash boxes and had a grater which fitted into the lid. Yet others, made in the late 18th and throughout the 19th centuries, consisted of a column of boxes which screwed into each other (some of these were made of sycamore in Sussex). Each compartment is labelled and after careful study the collector should be able to date the boxes by the style of labelling and finishing: 18th-century examples have script lettering on scrolled labels, those from the early 19th century have printed lettering on scrolled labels and Victorian examples printing on straight labels. The earlier examples usually had a well-rubbed-down varnished finish, later ones a poor varnish which scratched easily. Collectors should take care as some examples of later date have been stripped and refinished.

Illustrated opposite is a very elegant Georgian spice grater in lignum vitae. This hardwood was expensive and was reserved for the best examples. Spice grinders work on the same principle as coffee mills and have grinding-cogs of hand-forged steel. Grinders were made of many woods, including walnut, mahogany, maplewood and oak. Collectors of these items should aim for variety of shape and type of wood.

William-and-Mary oak spice cupboard with drawers; late 17th century. On top of it, right, is a 19th-century tiered set of spice boxes, and an 18th-century lignum vitae spice-grater.

Spice containers and nutmeg graters

American spice boxes followed the styles of boxes settlers had known in their homelands. English settlers kept up their tradition of comparatively plain wooden chests, nested boxes and japanned and tinned boxes. The Pennsylvania Dutch (who came from south-west Germany) continued to decorate their boxes with brightly-coloured painted patterns, as they did their furniture and general kitchenware. Illustrated in the Sears Roebuck mail-order catalogue of 1902 was an eight-drawer spice cabinet made of oil-finished ash; the drawers were labelled with their contents and it sold for 40 cents. A similarly-styled cabinet in polished hardwood and 'extra well finished' cost 42 cents. Some of these circular boxes have a grater in the centre, and rectangular japanned boxes often have a small grater which slides into runners on the inside of the deep lid.

Nutmeg graters were sometimes fitted above a drawer which caught the spice as it was ground. Box graters were very inexpensive. An unusual nutmeg grater advertised in the mail-order catalogue was listed as 'The Improved Edgar Nutmeg Grater' and described as follows: 'It will not clog, tear the fingers nor drop the nutmeg. It grates the nutmeg very fine, distributes it evenly and grates it all up.' This grater was fitted with a holder for the nutmeg which ran backwards and forwards on a piece of metal fixed to the grater—and this cost only eight cents!

Before the era of mass-production, many of these small items were made by local craftsmen.

Top: to bottom: late 19th-century spice box; early 20th-century spice-holder; mid-19th-century nutmeg graters.

Gadgets used in British kitchens

The industrial revolution in England brought increased consumer demand and the beginnings of mass-production. Manufacturers were full of ideas for new products, right down to small household items and there were plenty of cheap books, papers and catalogues to advertise the new gadgets.

As early as 1807 one Thomas Saddington had preserved fruit by putting it into wide-mouthed jars with loose-fitting lids, then standing them in a bath and heating them to 160 to 170 degrees Fahrenheit for about an hour; after this they were filled to the brim with hot water and tightly closed. Only about five years later Donkin and Hall established a factory for canning foods in Blue Anchor Road, Bermondsey, in south-east London. Preserving and canning meat, vegetables and fruit is a tedious operation, and mechanical aids such as pea-shellers must have been a great help. In 1860 a firm called Lyon, was advertising in the *Ironmonger Trades Gazette* such gadgets as the 'Improved Sausage Machine, shown at the Dublin Exhibition and won two prizes at the Paris Universal Exhibition of 1853'; a 'Shilling Cucumber, Potato and Onion Slicer'; 'Lyons New Suet Chopping Board and Knife: Root and Vegetable Pulpers'; and 'Hot or Cold Food Masticators—to assist Digestion due to loss of teeth, with or without hot water bottles to keep the food hot'.

Egg-beaters were a late-19th-century innovation. A recipe from 1655 for 'cream with snow' suggests that the egg whites should be beaten with 'a cleft stick or a bundle of reeds tied together and rolled between your hands standing upright in your cream'. Nearly two hundred years later the only improvement on that method was the use of a fork, and so egg-beaters really were a big advance. In the Harrods Catalogue of 1895 wire whisks were advertised starting at 4d.; patent egg-whisks with interlocking metal circles and cog-wheel drive cost 6½d.

It is an interesting sidelight on the reversal of earlier England to America trans-Atlantic trade that this beater used in an English kitchen was made in America.

Above: pea-sheller, made by A. Lyon of Finsbury, London; early 20th century. Below: Dover egg-beater, which carried patents ranging in date from 1873 to 1891, and which was made in the U.S.A. by the Dover Stamping Company.

Forks, racks and cheese graters

These long-handled forks, which make very attractive collectors' items, were usually made by country craftsmen. They had two uses: to hold food roasting over or in front of an open fire and to toast both bread and meat. Made in iron, steel or brass they range from the rare Elizabethan examples through elegant Queen Anne and Georgian forks to late 19th-century examples; the style of handles and terminals shows great individuality. Seventeenth- and 18th-century flesh or ham forks, with two or three prongs, evolved from the three-barbed flesh hook of Roman times.

One variation of the toasting-fork is a rack with two prongs joined to the end of a wooden handle. In one common form of the 18th-century toasting fork the three prongs are staggered to hold the bread more firmly. Some four-pronged forks of Scottish origin show continental influence in their profusion of decorative detail, which is not characteristic of English smithcraft. A Victorian brass 'lazy toaster' had a swivelled arm like a modern angle-poise lamp. Cooks' forks with two prongs were advertised in the Harrods Catalogue of 1895 in various sizes, at prices between 1s. 1d. and 2 shillings.

Eating-forks did not come into general use until the end of the 17th century—country folk felt that they did not need 'little forks to make hay with our mouths to throw our meat into them'. Queen Elizabeth and some of her nobles, however, are known to have bought quantities of steel forks at 7s. 6d. per dozen.

It was only in the late 18th century that technical difficulties in producing a third prong in the steel fork were overcome with the development of a treadle hammer known as an oliver. In the 17th century, the handles of table forks were cast in halves.

Cheese-graters are very interesting collectors' items and are a class of kitchen utensil, the design of which has changed little over a long period of time. One of the practical aspects of collecting kitchenware is that many of the best 'gadgets' or cookery aids have been around for some time, and graters, in particular, have a classic appearance. This cheese-grater in sheet brass could easily be used today, as long as it is kept clean and shiny and dried carefully after use.

Selection of long-handled forks, ranging from Elizabethan in date to the late 19th century; fork rack surmounted by birds and animals, late 18th century; brass cheese-grater, dated 1788.

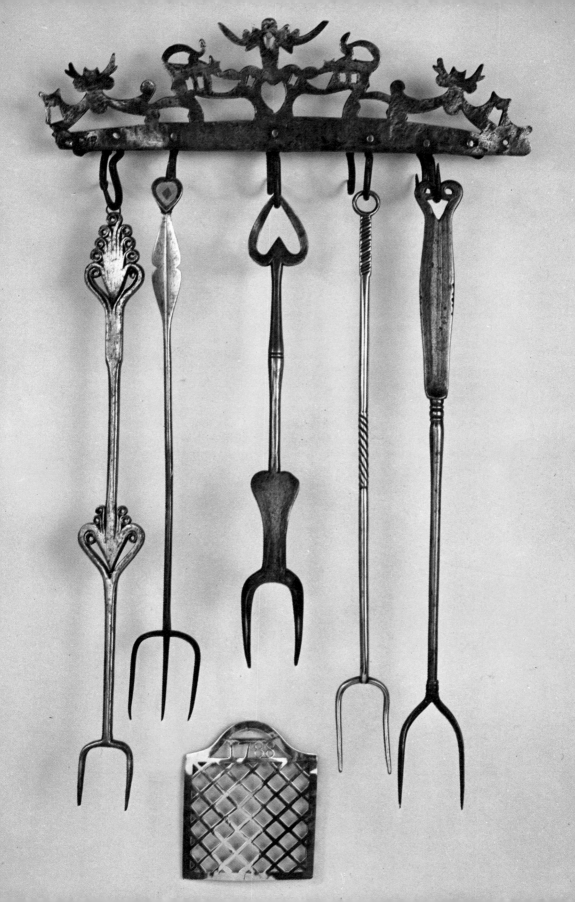

Canisters

In early colonial times people who lived in isolated rural areas made few shopping trips. Though they were self-supporting on the whole, they had to buy some things, such as sugar, rice, dried fruits, etc. These they purchased in large quantities, perhaps even by the barrel. As transport improved and towns grew, it became possible to make more frequent shopping trips and buy smaller quantities of fresh goods. In England stoneware and earthenware crocks and jars had been made for a long time, principally in Staffordshire and Nottingham, but also in other areas. In America stoneware and salt-glazed earthenware was made at Bennington in Vermont and at a number of potteries in New England and New York State, where the best known include the Clark Pottery of Athens, and Whitman of Havana, New York and Albany, New York. One of the distinctive types of decoration consisted of incised patterns filled in with cobalt blue; designs were usually lively, naive drawings of animals and foliage. Canisters were also made of tin and in Victorian times these were enamelled or 'japanned' for greater decorative effect. The Pennsylvania Dutch were particularly fond of brightly-coloured and decorated kitchenware. Much of the japanning was done by women, and in Connecticut a number of tin-smithing families still have records listing the women who worked for them.

Earthenware preserves jar, 1910; enamel raisin jar, 19th century; pottery starch container, 19th century.

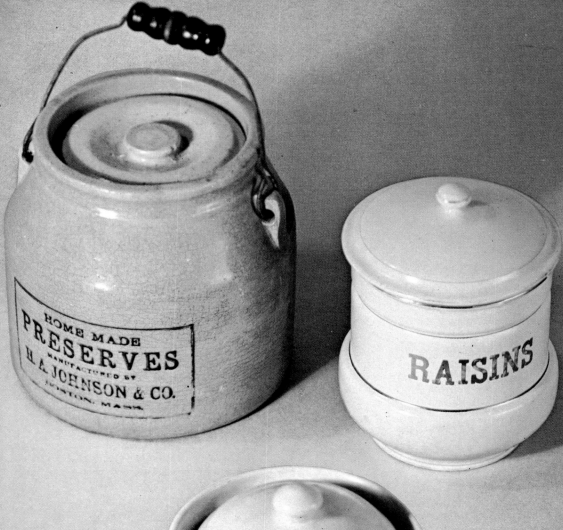

Gadgets used in American kitchens

'Labour-saving' gadgets were unknown in Victorian times, when servants were plentiful and cheap. But as the number of jobs in factories grew and women became more emancipated, servants grew less easy to find. This made such gadgets all the more welcome; international exhibitions and women's magazines promoted them, and expanding factory output, improved transport and an efficient sales network brought the goods to the customer.

The Dover egg-beater was patented in 1873. In 1900 the Holts Patent Egg-Beater was one of the favourite types; it was a hand-held mixer, the blades moving in opposite directions one within the other. Cheaper spoon-shaped egg-beaters were also on sale, retailing for as little as two cents. An early electric mixer and beater was made by Landers, Friary and Clark of New Britain, Connecticut, who were famous for their range of household appliances. This machine was hinged so that it could be used both horizontally and vertically, and many extra attachments were available.

The potato peeler, which also dates from the late 19th century, was another way of reducing time spent on laborious tasks. Advertised at the turn of the century were similar devices, among them a 'rotary-knife family peach and apple parer', a 'rocking table apple parer with clamp', a 'potato-and-food-slicer with knives of tempered steel' and an 'apple parer, corer and slicer combined'. There were even cherry-stoners (sold under the trade names of Enterprise and Rollman) and 'Raisin & Grape Seeders'.

The soap-shaver was an economical way of using up small left-over ends of soap. Ice was kept in blocks wrapped in flannel, and an ice-shaver was used to chip them down. The smaller pieces of ice were packed into tub-shaped ice-cream freezers and around double-compartment ice-cream moulds.

Top to bottom: Soap-shaver, c. 1910; egg-beater, c. 1886; ice-shaver, early 20th century; potato-peeler, c. 1884.

Innovations by the late 19th century

This model of a late 19th-century kitchen provides us with an interesting example of how technology had progressed from the beginning of the century and how, in some ways, things had altered very little. The greatest change is the use of gas for lighting and cooking. There is a 'Black Beauty' gas cooker made by R & A Main in about 1878 which certainly must have been the pride of the kitchen in which it was first installed. It has four large drilled-tube burners, the oven is brick lined and its non-aerated burner burns on all four sides. The range, which was called The Quadrant Double-oven Kitchen Range was made by William Willett, in about 1890. The central coal fire was flanked by two ovens and the heat could be regulated by quadrants over each, these worked slides which opened or closed the flues. Pots and pans were heated over holes in the cast iron top. Sometimes these stoves had a 'hot water back' or tank behind the fire to supply domestic hot water—it would have cost £16 in those days. However, this kitchen shows only a cold water tap at the sink—and even this would have been unusual outside the large towns. The kettle on the hob and hot water cans would have been filled for use in the bedrooms.

However, there are already gadgets making their appearance to lighten the tedium of some of the household chores: a mincing machine which clamps on to the table; an apple and potato parer and peeler, which also clamps on to the table; a cake mixer with a cranked handle which works two revolving blades; a bread and meat slicer, and a knife cleaner. Advertising had also found its way into the kitchen by this time. There is a blancmange mould of white glazed earthenware with a recipe by Brown & Polson, a stoneware jar for Keiller marmalade, a stoneware jug for E. W. Taylor's mineral water and a calendar advertising the mineral waters of J. B. Bowler of Corn Street, Bath.

The religious text 'God is our refuge and our strength' is typical of the Victorian moral rectitude, but the hardworked servant must have wondered where either refuge or strength were to be found in the midst of her constant round of work.

Reconstruction of late 19th-century British kitchen.

Teapots

Tea came to England in 1660 but was at first an expensive luxury. During the 18th century it became more and more popular and when duty was reduced from four shillings to one shilling in 1745, consumption trebled. In 1852 duty was paid on 54,724,615 pounds of tea and in addition a considerable amount was smuggled into the country.

Teapots are very interesting items of kitchenware to collect, for there is an almost endless variety of shapes and types of decoration. There is only space to deal with pottery and porcelain examples here, although kitchen teapots were made in other materials. Many of the teapots made recently for general use can be purchased quite cheaply. Normally there will be no indication as to where they were made, and it is quite a challenge to learn what shapes and patterns each factory produced. Pattern books kept by factories still survive and it is sometimes possible to identify a piece from them. Remember too that condition affects price and that these days repairs can be extremely skilful and difficult for the novice to detect.

Manufacture of porcelain teapots in America only started in the 19th century, copying porcelain imported from France and England. Early teapots in America were of earthenware, often with a coloured glaze. Manganese produced a black, glossy surface, and on a redware base the homely black teapot was a familiar sight in most kitchens. These simpler wares are seldom marked. Tuckers of Philadelphia produced much fine tableware, as did Knowles, Taylor and Knowles of Ohio, and the Jersey City Porcelain Company copied English wares and produced Rockingham-type brown-glazed pottery. Greenpoint of Brooklyn, New Jersey, later known as Union Porcelain Works, made both hard and soft paste until the end of the century. Styles ranged from the simple 18th-century globular shapes, based on Chinese originals, through the sometimes florid shapes of the 19th century to the simple, flowing lines of Art Deco in the 1920s.

American Art Deco teapot, by Hall, early 20th century.

Tea-strainers

To cater for the enormous popularity of tea-drinking, large numbers of tea sets were manufactured, from beautiful porcelain and silver sets at the luxury end of the trade to ordinary earthenware and tin ones at the other end. The two strainers shown opposite are both of European origin and were made in the early 20th century. The porcelain example might have been used in the drawing room with a prettily-painted tea service. The Staffordshire potteries turned out vast quantities of such services for home use and for export. The wire strainer was for everyday and kitchen use; in 1902 Sears Roebuck advertised a very similar strainer as 'extra fine wire gauge with enamelled handle'; these came in three sizes and ranged in price from 5 cents for the small size to 8 cents for the larger size. A pure aluminium example was advertised as 'just fitting over an ordinary size cup, 12 cents'.

Another type of strainer was a 'spout strainer' which was attached to the spout of the teapot. There were also 'tea or coffee balls'; these were made of tinned wire with a hinge and catch. The tea or coffee was put in the ball and then in the pot, and the mail-order catalogue claimed that the full strength of the beverage was obtained without grounds or leaves and that a strainer was not necessary—an early example of a 'convenience' gadget.

Tea-strainers: European porcelain strainer, c. 1910; German wire strainer, 1910.

Coffee-grinders

It should be easy for the collector to find a great variety of coffee mills or grinders. In the 18th century coffee was an expensive luxury drink, and so, of course, grinders were expensive and elegant too. They were upright and looked like tall round boxes, although they did vary in shape—they might be cylindrical, or vase- or urn-shaped. The screw-on top had a crank handle; the beans were put into the top compartment or grinding chamber and the grounds passed into the bottom chamber, which was also threaded. Grinders were generally made of lignum vitae, although other woods were used.

In the 19th century, when coffee was more popular, grinders became everyday objects. The scoop which took the beans was made either of iron or of brass and a drawer beneath caught the ground coffee. Mass-production and cheaper transport and the birth of the mail-order business in America in the early 1870s helped to bring such items into every household. The following models were advertised in the early years of the 20th century: a canister coffee mill, made of japanned tin, the canister holding one pound of coffee; 'X-ray' coffee mill, with wood frame and hopper and glass front—this was easily regulated, and was intended for fixing on a wall; jewel coffee mill, with heavy ornamental glass canister, capacity graduated —this had the latest grinding burrs, while the iron parts were finished in red enamel; the appliance was packed in a wooden box.

Iron coffee-grinder; early 20th century.

Toasters

Early toasters were made for use on the down hearth, in front of an open fire. Of iron, with a long handle, swivelled onto a stand on each side of which were two semi-circular hoops about an inch apart, they looked like a forerunner of a modern toast-rack. The bread or meat was put between the hoops and could be turned without touching the food. Another method of toasting was a salamander. This was a metal disc with a long handle, which was put into the fire until red hot and then held close to the bread. The salamander was also used for browning the top of a dish without cooking it further—Eliza Acton describes one in her book *Modern Cookery*.

Of course, the simplest method of toasting was to put a piece of bread on a long-handled fork and hold it in front of the fire. A German visitor to England in 1782 was intrigued with 'toast' and described it as follows: 'But there is another kind of bread and butter usually eaten with tea, which is toasted by the fire and is incomparably good. You take one slice after the other and hold it to the heat till the butter is melted so that it penetrates a number of slices, this is called toast.' One type of American toasting-fork was mounted on a small stand and for as long as cooking took place either over or in front of an open fire this was the only method of toasting. Wire toasters advertised in the early part of the 20th century had a long wooden handle and two wire squares between which the bread was held before the fire. The 'Crown Asbestos Toaster' was described in a mail-order catalogue thus: 'Asbestos disc covered with steel wire cloth, the lower surface being covered with sheet steel. Has a corrugated steel rim and always-cool Alaska handle. For toasting bread, rusks or crackers on gas, gasoline or coal stove it is fine. Can also be used under cooking utensils to keep from scorching.'

One of the first electric toasters was made by the General Electric Company in 1913. It had four vertical elements mounted on a porcelain base with a heavy wire rack to hold the bread. But as with electric irons there was no thermostat and this was a serious drawback.

Toaster, for use over a flame on the stove (the bread had to be turned by hand); c. 1910.

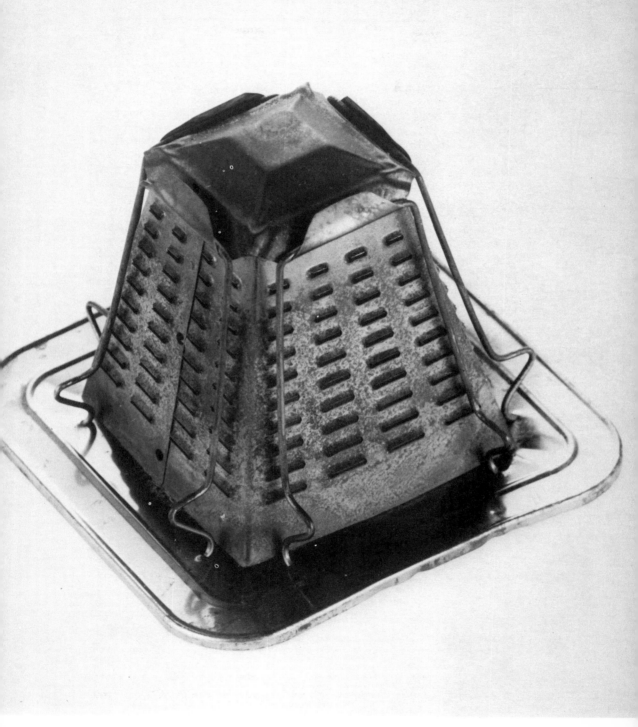

Ladles and skimmers

Skimmers are of two types: the most common had a long iron handle attached to a circular pan of brass, copper or tinned iron, the surface of which was perforated with small round holes. The second type, known as a 'flit', had a small ring handle. Skimmers were used in dairies to take the cream off the top of the milk and also in the kitchen to remove scum and fat from cauldrons of boiling meat and vegetables. Deep-bowled spoons were used only for ladling. Utensils with flexible metal blades were employed for turning scones and oatcakes on gridirons.

Not only were items such as these made by a local smith, they were also sent back to him for repair. In the Blacksmith's Ledgers for 1736 to 1773 of the Hedges family from Bucklebury in Berkshire skimmers and ladles are noted as having been sent for repair. We still have records of some 18th-century foundries: the Rudhall family in Salisbury were bellmakers, and James Keene of Woodstock and Joshua Kipling of Portsmouth made saucepans and, no doubt, a wide range of metal implements as well.

Also of interest to collectors are spoons and ladles made of wood, sometimes known as treenware. These utilitarian objects were usually simply shaped and carved in beech, lime and sycamore. Racks to hold them were also carved. In the second half of the 18th century young men would carve a wooden spoon and decorate its handle with love symbols; these spoons became known as 'love spoons' and were especially popular in North Wales. Some were certainly made for use by the loved one in her kitchen, though the especially ornamental ones were obviously meant as keepsakes.

Top: late-18th-century brass colander. Centre, left to right: early-18th-century (George II) brass ladle riveted to wrought-iron handle with typical suspension hook; 19th-century bread-hook; large skimmer with owner's initials and William-and-Mary royal cypher beneath a crown; 19th-century brass ladle; 19th-century brass skimmer; late-18th-century copper meat fork. Below: 19th-century brass skimmer.

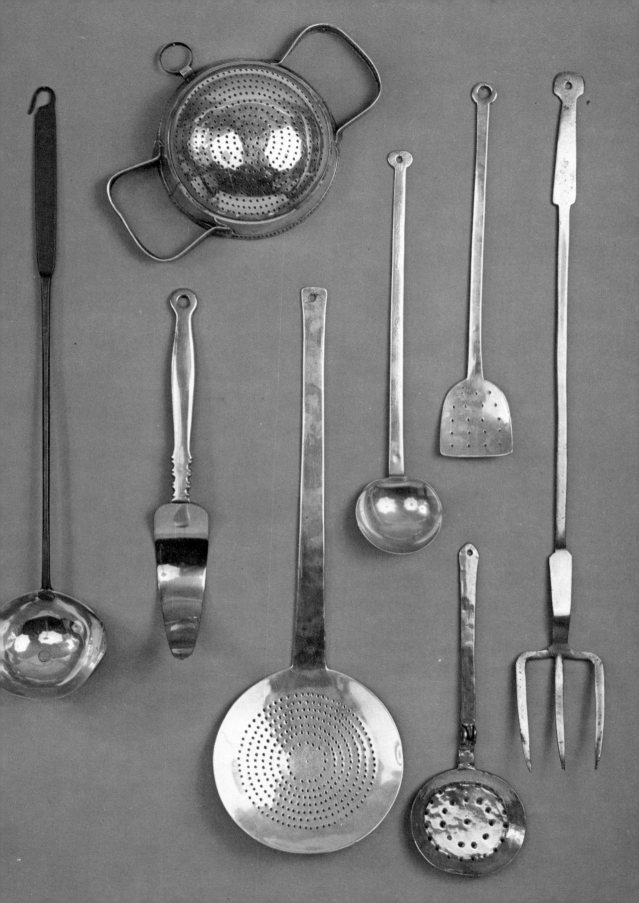

Ice-cream scoops

The first ice-creams to be made were packed into moulds and frozen in ice-caves and ice-chests. It was soon found, however, that churning or beating the ice-cream in a freezer improved the texture a great deal. An American lady, one Nancy Johnson, is reputed to have invented the first ice-cream freezer in 1864. Mrs Marshall, who ran a cookery school in Mortimer Street, London, published a *Book of Ices* in 1885 which illustrated an ice-cream freezer and gave full details of how to use it. She gave a number of recipes for ice-creams, water ices, mousse, iced souffles and 'dressed ices' and illustrated a great variety of copper moulds in the form of various fruits, asparagus, wheatsheaf, as well as some fancy moulds in pewter.

The earliest freezers consisted of a wooden tub containing an inner box which could be cranked like a butter churn. Next came a metal cylinder inside a wooden pail with a handle that worked a paddle. The 'Star' ice-cream freezer was made of whitewood with a tin cylinder, the 'Paragon' of oak with a pewter cylinder and the 'Glaciator' was a flatter tub also with a paddle. Shepard's 'Lighting' machine was advertised in the Sears Roebuck Catalogue of 1902 and both this and the 'American' freezer were marketed in England. Spongs made a freezer which consisted of a metal cylinder mounted horizontally on a stand. Collectors should also look out for other items used in making ice-cream—sugar-thermometers, palette knives, caramel-cutters, sugar-scrapers and sugar-droppers.

Ice-cream scoops like those illustrated were advertised in Sears Roebuck's 1902 Catalogue as 'Ice Cream Disher having two revolving knives which cut the cream loose. By one half turn of the button the cream slips out a smooth and perfect cone'. They cost as little as ten cents. Sizes indicate number of dishes to the quart.

An American pictorial advertisement of about 1880 for a small city drugstore shows a soda fountain on a side counter. By the turn of the century the soda fountain had become a major institution in American life. These were elaborate and elegant marble monuments with scores of spigots and wells and a delightfully confusing variety of ices and syrups.

The first ice-cream was probably made in China and then in Rome. In the 1880s, Neopolitan ice-cream was considered the ideal, but 'Philadelphia' was not far behind, and American housewives were leaders of the world in flavourings and finely textured creams.

Three ice-cream scoops; c. 1900.

Nutcrackers

Nutcrackers have been used in Europe since at least the 16th century—indeed Henry VIII is known to have presented a pair to Anne Boleyn. Early nutcrackers were usually made of wood; some of the finest were manufactured in France, often of boxwood and usually in the form of a human figure, the lower jaw being hinged to the back handle so that it dropped open to hold the nut when the handles were opened. Towards the middle of the 17th century a single cracker without hand pieces but with a screw action came into use. The double-handled varieties were revived in the 18th century, however, and metal was substituted for wood; luxury silver-plated crackers were even made. Some of the early wooden nutcrackers are fine specimens of the carver's art. One particularly attractive example I once saw was made of hazelnut in the form of a squirrel; the nut was placed in a hole in the squirrel's belly and the handle screwed up to crush the nut.

By the Victorian era brass had become popular, and the nut-crackers shown opposite are all brass. In 1780 James Emerson had fused zinc and copper in the ratio of one to two and produced a very high-quality brass; ten years later the Waterbury Brass Works opened in Connecticut. By the early 19th century trade directories were listing makers of brass and wrought iron; occasionally manufacturers would mark their work with an impressed mark. Thus W. H. Pries of Canal Street, New York, who is listed in the New York directories of the 1830s, devised a trivet of brass and iron.

Nuts formed part of the dessert course and so nutcrackers were required in the dining room as well as in the kitchen, where they were used extensively before the advent of 'convenience' packs of shelled nuts!

Three brass nutcrackers, all Victorian; the squirrel motif is obvious, the legs all too suggestive, and the eagle clearly chosen for its appeal to patriotic Americans.

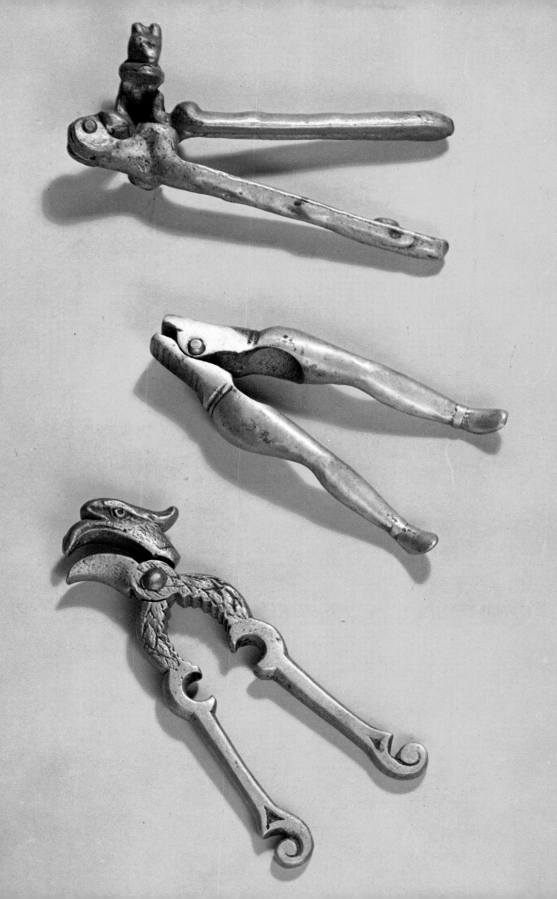

Scales

Scales were in common use in country stores where so many commodities had to be weighed out from sacks and barrels. Thus there were grocery store scales, with heavy brass scoops, dairy scales, advertised 'with Butter Salter Attachment' and as 'scaled carefully with the United States standard and . . . absolutely correct', and platform counter scales. For the customer who wanted to see for herself that she was not being cheated the 'Agate Bearing Butcher Counter Scales' were available; the dial could be seen from both sides, and the scales had a 'fine nickel-plated sash, agate bearing, black enamelled base and marble slab'. There were also simple spring balances, some of which had a dial and a hook, others a measure and a tin dish.

In 1896 Mrs D. A. Lincoln, one of the original authors of the *Boston Cooking School Cook Book,* now generally known as *Fannie Farmer*, began to rationalize kitchen measurements. She felt that terms such as 'a pinch of salt' and 'nuts' of butter were insufficiently accurate. The precise measuring system that we take for granted today was launched with the publication of the *Boston Cook Book.* The early 20th-century 'Acme Household Scale' weighed up to 20 lbs. by ounces; it had a tin scoop and a brass dial. The manufacturers' claim was that: 'It will detect mistakes (intentional or otherwise) in weighing articles you buy. Every farmer and every family should by all means have one or more scales.' The 'American Family Scales', advertised in 1902, were described as follows: 'Made of steel with steel top, white enamelled dial. Weighs 24 lbs. by ounces. Occupies little space, is light and easily moved. Regulated by brass screw on top. It is a convenient scale to use and has no weights that can be lost. You can look this one in the face to prove its accuracy without looking for weights.' Once again the word convenient crops up, a sign of the increasing freedom of women from kitchen drudgery.

None-the-less, the earlier scales with brass or copper bowls balanced by a set of weights have great charm, and have been a collectors' item for many years. There is a bewildering variety of shapes and sizes and, if the weights are complete, they can be useful as well as ornamental.

American family cooking scales, 1920; and English brass scales with weights, late 19th century.

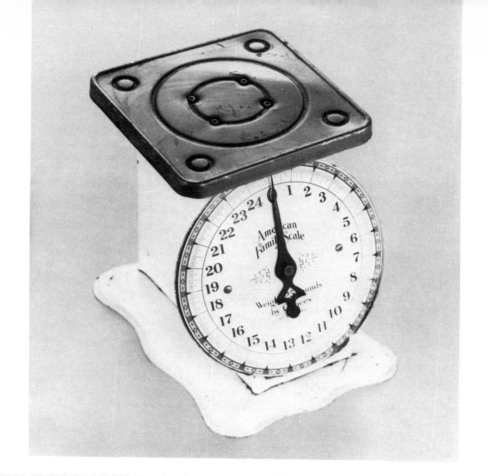

Blue-and-white printed earthenware

Blue-and-white transfer-printed earthenware was produced in vast quantities in the early 19th century in the Staffordshire potteries and also in Yorkshire, Lancashire, Northumberland and South Wales. The standard of printing was good and most households must have boasted some blue-and-white dishes on their dressers. Vast quantities were exported from Britain—especially to America; many of these pieces bore American views. Literally thousands of different patterns were produced, and although patterns by famous potters can be expensive, most plates and dishes can still be acquired for a modest price.

Blue-printing on earthenware started in Britain in 1780 and until the beginning of the 19th century almost all the patterns were inspired by imported Chinese porcelain. They are extremely varied and only gradually became standardized in the well-known 'willow pattern'. Apart from plates and dishes, jugs, mugs, all the various soup, sauce and vegetable tureens, gravy boats and stands were made, as well as tea, coffee, dessert and supper services.

Many different themes can inspire collections of blue-and-white earthenware: marked pieces either of the wares of one particular factory or of as many different factories as possible; different versions of patterns—for instance 'chinoiserie' patterns, inspired by Chinese porcelain, or topographical patterns copied from contemporary book illustrations of named views of castles, country houses, famous abbeys and churches, or American views intended for export. The gardener-collector might search for floral or botanical patterns based on some of the fine prints in period botanical publications (the best known are Wedgwood's Botanical Flowers patterns), the animal-lover for patterns with identifiable birds and animals—Adams, Spode, Rogers and Stevenson all produced patterns of this kind and Job Meigh produced a series called Zoological Sketches. Historical events (a well-known series was made by Jones & Son) and commemorative patterns were also reproduced.

Spode blue-and-white fish dish; 19th-century. The potter had to use his print one-and-a-half times to cover the surface.

Openers

Corkscrews first appeared at the end of the 17th century; their use grew as the practice of maturing bottled wine in bins grew. If wine was to be kept for any length of time, the cork had to be kept moist to preserve the seal and so it was best to store the bottles on their side, and the cork itself had to be very tight-fitting and pushed well-home to prevent leakage. The bottlescrew or corkscrew thus became indispensable.

Most collectable corkscrews date from the 19th century since earlier examples were mostly made in silver and fall outside the limits of inexpensive kitchenware. First patent rights were obtained by Samuel Henshall in 1795. The next to bring out a patent was Edward Thomason of Birmingham in 1802—a double-action mechanism incorporating a hermaphrodite screw. This type was popular well into the 20th century and was made by a number of firms including James Heeley, Barlow, Robert Jones and Dowler. In 1838 Thomas Lund of London patented an addition to the corkscrew—steel springs which held the upper end of the neck of the bottle.

A number of patents followed in the middle of the 19th century. William Lund of London patented two in 1855, which were in production for a long time. They were the 'London Rack' and 'Lund's Lever'. Numbers of firms made corkscrews, including Weiss of London, Evans, Looker, Retton, Mapplebeck & Lowe, Lowcock and Samuel Cotterill. The 'Tangent Lever' was registered in 1873 by Edwin Wolverston and made by James Heeley of Birmingham. It continued in production until the 1920s—the price then was 20s. a dozen. A rare corkscrew is the 'Holborn Lever' patented in 1885, and in the early 1870s an inexpensive wire corkscrew was invented in America by William Rockwell Clough.

Many corkscrews had ivory or bone handles as well as wooden ones, and some were fitted with a brush at one end of the handle for dusting the neck of the bottle.

Bottle openers also offer a wide range. The screw cap was invented in 1858 by John Landis Mason and the metal crown seal in 1892 by William Painter; the early 1900s brought a variety of openers for lifting off the crown seal. These came with many different 'ends'.

Can or tin openers are particularly interesting as they can often be dated by their patent. The 'Peerless' and 'Delmonic' were patented in 1890, the 'Neverslip' in 1892, and in 1920 the Star Can Opener Company of San Francisco patented a thumbscrew can opener.

Four Victorian openers: corkscrew and bottle-opener with dog's-head handles in carved wood; brass bottle-opener in the form of a fish; iron can-opener in the form of a buffalo-head.

Bowls

Earthenware was an inexpensive material, suitable for kitchen utensils which were used a good deal and liable to be broken. Bowls of the type shown opposite were made over a period of time in both England and America. England exported much earthenware from her potteries in Staffordshire to America, especially blue-printed wares made in the middle of the 19th century. Soon the colonists made their own, however, copying the styles that were popular. Potteries sprang up wherever there was clay of suitable quality, especially in Philadelphia and New Jersey. In 1826 William Ellis Tucker started making porcelain in Philadelphia. This firm produced all the dinnerware for the Hotel Touraine in Boston. In 1828 David Henderson took over the Jersey City Porcelain and Earthenware Company (it had first gone into production two years before); it copied English wares and made much stoneware, creamware and yellowware. The U.S. Pottery Company of Bennington, Vermont made much utilitarian ware with various glazes.

For collectors of typically American earthenware the outstanding styles are the Pennsylvania German sgraffito ware (sgraffito describes the process by which a coloured clay slip is superimposed on another and the design scratched through the outer coating) and slipware-decorated dishes, plates, jars, etc. A fine collection can be seen at the Henry Francis du Pont Winterthur Museum, Delaware.

Kitchen bowls were the poor cousins of the pottery industry and were often in plain red, white and yellow ware with simple glazes. Often made in local kilns, their charm is in a sturdy, 'country' feeling which concentrated on function rather than decoration. But by the mid-19th century, Victorian embellishment took over even here and bowls often matched the rest of the kitchen equipment, with transfer prints, in blue and black especially stripes of colour, and sometimes more practical decoration such as quantity lines or notations (3 pints, 2 quarts, etc.).

Look for unchipped rims and marks which would help to establish date and place of manufacture.

Earthenware bowls, top to bottom: c. *1890,* c. *1860, and* c. *1800.*

Recipe books

Old recipe books are a mine of fascinating information not only about cookery but also about many aspects of social history.

There are two kinds of recipe books—those printed for sale and those hand-written by the lady of the household, who kept in a book treasured 'receipts' for cooking and wine-making, medical recipes and cosmetic formulae. Some of these family books were kept by successive generations for over a century.

Obviously, old books which still have all their plates command a high price; a recipe book which has lost some of its plates may be less expensive, and its 'receipts' will still appeal to the collector of kitchenware.

There are some early recipe books dating from the 17th and 18th centuries, but although marvellous to read, they are mostly far too rare and expensive for the average collector.

The late Victorian age saw a revolution in the kitchen, hundreds of new books were issued from about 1870 onwards, and are available today for quite moderate prices. Look for illustrated ones that are complete; most domestic books have been well used and are unlikely to be in mint condition. Read about the most popular writers (Mrs Beeton, Fannie Farmer) and look for first editions if possible. They can still be found quite cheaply and must increase rapidly in value. The outer covering is not important as long as the book is complete.

They can illustrate more than food—the model American butcher of 1905 refers with pride to a 'range of the latest pattern, and sinks with hot and cold water'—salutary reminders of how far we have moved in comparatively few years. An earlier ice cream book (1886), written by 'an American' and dedicated to the housekeepers of America, lists everything you need and describes every utensil—'tinned graters are now made flat, of fine tin plate, thickly perforated with star-shaped holes, and stretched upon wooden frames strong and durable.' Referring to measures, the author says that 'a late invented measure of tapering form is marked with rings on shoulders at different heights . . . from a gill to a quart'.

This sort of information is absolutely invaluable to a collector of kitchenware.

Frontispiece and title page of 18th-century book of Receipts of Pastry and Cookery *by Edward Kidder, pastry-master.*

Rob. Sheppard Sculp.

EDW. KIDDER
Pastry-master.

E. Kidder's
RECEIPTS
OF
Pastry
AND
Cookery
For the Use of his Scholars.

Who teaches at his School in
St. Martins le Grand:
On Mondays, Tuesdays & Wednesdays,
In the Afternoon.
ALSO
On Thursdays, Fridays & Saturdays,
In the Afternoon,
at his School next to
Furnivals Inn in Holborn.

*Ladies may be taught at
their own Houses.*

Knife-cleaning machines

Today it is hard to imagine the drudgery of cleaning table silver and steel cutlery, once a weekly job in all but the poorest households. A thick paste made from hartshorn powder and spirits of wine was left on the plate for some time and then brushed off and polished with special 'plate rags'. These were made 'from the tops of old cotton stockings', which were boiled in a mixture of new milk and hartshorn powder in the proportion of an ounce of powder to a pint of milk for five minutes and then dried before the fire. Careful cleaning was essential to remove stains from steel cutlery. Originally the cutlery was scoured with a strong solution of common washing soda and water and then polished on a buff leather or india rubber mounted on a board. The cutlery was often stored in a box which hung by the fireside to preserve it from rust.

An advertisement issued in 1880 by Spong & Co. for 'The Servant's Friend Patent Knife Cleaner', must have been read with relief in many a kitchen. It claimed that 'The Servant's Friend does not belie its name, quickly imparting a lustrous polish to the knives'. By the end of the 19th century two kinds of polishing machine had been invented. The most common type was circular in shape. The knives were inserted into grooves on the side of a drum-shaped container mounted on a stand. The handle turned an inner wheel fitted with leather leaves; these plus an abrasive emery powder cleaned and stropped the knives.

In 1882 Kents' patent knife-cleaner consisted of a wooden drum mounted vertically on a cast-iron stand. It looked like a miniature mangle with a revolving india rubber roller which, it was claimed, 'gives a beautiful silver-like polish to the blades without wearing them away, or causing any damage whatever to the handles'. Between four and eight knives could be cleaned in one minute, shoulders and back included. By the 1890s Kents had produced their less expensive 'Improved Patent' model.

In their Catalogue, Harrods highly recommended two cheaper versions, one of which was the Davis 'Excelsior', the other the 'Spong Patent Self-adjusting Stag', illustrated here.

Patent knife-cleaning machine—the 'Self-adjusting Stag' (with polish) made by Spong and Co. Ltd; late 19th and early 20th centuries.

Cleaning the house

Cleaning the house has always been an integral part of housekeeping and yields some interesting collector's items. Methods of cleaning did not change for centuries, and hand-made brooms and brushes were used until they wore out. These were the 'badges' of house-servants, who would carry them as a sign of their trade at country 'mop fairs' when they were looking for a job.

The Industrial Revolution and the flood of inventions in the 19th century brought a revolution in cleaning methods, however. In 1840 the engineer Sir Joseph Whitworth patented a sweeper with revolving brushes; these are still used in carpet sweepers today. The greatest innovation was the vacuum cleaner, invented by the English civil engineer A. Cecil Booth in 1901. The first examples were mounted on horse-drawn cabs; uniformed employees of the Vacuum Cleaner Co. passed the suction pipes through the windows. So novel were they that in the early years of the 20th century fashionable London hostesses gave tea-parties at which the main entertainment was to watch the cleaners at work.

Domestic vacuum cleaners were first manufactured in 1904, and the servant shortage after the First World War made them very popular. There are several notable models still around. The electric vacuum cleaner was invented in America in 1908 by James Spangler, a member of the Hoover family. A significant innovation was its external dust bag and compact fan unit. The Baby Daisy, an English machine of 1910 with double-acting bellows, worked by a wooden handle attached to one of the bellows; a connecting rod operated the other. The cloth dust bag is horizontal on the side. Two servants were required to operate it, and it cost £4. The Star vacuum cleaner of 1911 was hand-operated by one person; it worked on the principle of the bicycle pump, but in reverse; dust was collected in the cylinder. Other important types include the B.V.C. hand-operated vacuum cleaner of 1912; the 'Cyclone' hand-operated vacuum cleaner of 1914; and the 'Daisy' sweeper of 1914, in which the wheels pumped a double-action bellows; a cloth dust bag was inside a box at the back.

Above: B.V.C. hand-operated vacuum cleaner; c. 1912. Below: Baby Daisy vacuum cleaner; 1910.

Flat-iron stands

In the 18th and 19th centuries ironing was done either on a dresser or on a large kitchen table. Stands were necessary for the hot, heavy irons to prevent them burning the ironing cloth. Like the irons, the stands were probably in pairs. Most of the stands that a collector will come across today date from the 19th century. Made in brass, bell metal, steel or bronze, their designs varied considerably, although they were usually shaped like the flat base of an iron and supported on three or four feet. The simplest version was made in sheet steel with three peg legs and a pierced triangular top. A variant of this was cast in brass, pierced with a star and had heavy peg legs.

Other trivets, or tripods, were placed in the hearth to hold kettles and saucepans. Made of iron, early examples were simply shaped, later ones heavily decorated. Some stands had hooks so that they could be clipped over the bars of the grate and hold a pan or kettle near the heat. Some trivets also have a swivelling toasting-fork or an adjustable rest to hold the handle of a basting spoon. Trivets were probably made by the local blacksmith and so no maker's names appear.

Top row, left to right: brass stand pierced with keyhole design, c. 1820; unusual stand cast in bronze in form of cat's face, c. 1880; bell-metal stand with elaborate pierced top and double-scroll handle. Centre row, left and right: child's miniature iron stands, mid-19th century; between them a heart-shaped cut-steel stand. Bottom row, left to right: stand with naval (or masonic) design of square and compasses commemorating Battle of Trafalgar, 1805; unusual stand with design of fox and trees, 19th century; heart-shaped bronze stand with decorative piercing, possibly made as a love-token, 19th century.

Irons

How tedious ironing must have been when the heavy irons had to be heated either on or in front of an open fire or on a stove and when clothes had so many ruffles and pleats. Irons required wiping before use to clean them of soot and smoke. They were often called 'sad irons', the expression perhaps derived from the Old English word 'sald' meaning solid. They were sold in pairs and in some cases with detachable handles to protect the hands. A set of irons with this type of handle was invented by Mrs Potts in America in 1871; Sears Roebuck in their mail-order catalogue in 1902 advertised a similar set, with three irons with forged stretcher handles, a wooden detachable handle and a finely-polished iron stand. The set sold for 67 cents—73 cents if you wanted them nickel-plated.

Some irons were hollow and were heated with an iron slug, which had to be pre-heated in the fire and also with charcoal. The elaborate dresses fashionable in the 19th century required special irons—a sleeve or flounce iron, for instance; this also had a detachable handle. Crown hand fluters were for pleated garments. The plate rested on a japanned cast base and the heating iron cast on the bottom of the plate. The plate had to be removed, heated on the stove and returned to the base when hot. The handle and the yoke which held the roll were made of malleable iron, and all the unpolished parts were japanned. A large crown fluting machine had four heaters with a pair of tongs sold *en suite*. Polishing irons and Chinese laundry irons were also advertised. In 1889 a Mr Carpenter of St Paul, Minnesota invented an electric flat iron, and seven years later electric irons were available for the American home. General Electric produced a domestic electric iron in 1904, but these early electric products were difficult to regulate as thermostats were only invented much later. The 1930 'Mysto' model incorporated a thermostat. In fact, the real revolution in ironing came not with light, electric irons, but with non-iron fabrics!

Top to bottom: iron with wooden handle, late 19th century; iron with iron handle, late 19th century; miniature iron, early 20th century.

Irons for various uses

In the 18th century washing clothes was a laborious affair—in some houses it was done once every four or five weeks, in others once a quarter, and yet others had what was termed 'bucking'—a great wash three times a year. In the 19th century the washing-house was usually attached to the kitchen, the floor sloping towards a gutter connected with the drain. A range of wooden tubs, a boiler and a furnace were all that the room was equipped with! Though in modern times washing is often done by machines, ironing has changed very little and is generally still done by hand!

The collector will find that the great variety of irons makes this field very interesting. Most will probably date from the 19th century. This is Mrs Beeton's description, which may prove enlightening:— 'The irons consist of the common flat iron which is of different sizes varying from 4 to 10 inches in width at the broad end: the oval iron, which is used for more delicate articles and the box iron, which is hollow and heated by a red-hot iron inserted into the box.'

The collector may also come across the following models: 'Cannon' charcoal-heated iron with bellows (c. 1850)—the iron had a charcoal fire inside and a hole at the back through which the nozzle of the bellows was inserted; 'flat' irons heated on a stove or in front of a bright fire (c. 1850); 'self-heating box iron' made by Kents of London (c. 1862); a Wanzer pleating-iron, specially for making pleats (c. 1880); curved bottom-polishing irons with convex sole (c. 1880), used to produce a glazed finish on starched linen garments; spirit-heated travelling-irons (c. 1890) with iron, spirit stove, spirit container, matchbox and small folding ironing-board, all contained in a leather travelling case; Kenrick 'Bonus' Spirit Iron (c. 1900) which burned methylated spirits in a brass holder—the flame being directed onto the sole of the iron; gas-heated iron (c. 1930) with stand by the Davis Gas Stove Co. of Birmingham—this had an internal gas burner and was fitted with a hand-shield.

Left, top, a charcoal iron, with space inside for small charcoal fire; bottom, a goffering or 'Italian' iron. Right, two late-18th-century box irons—the heat came from the blocks previously heated and placed inside.

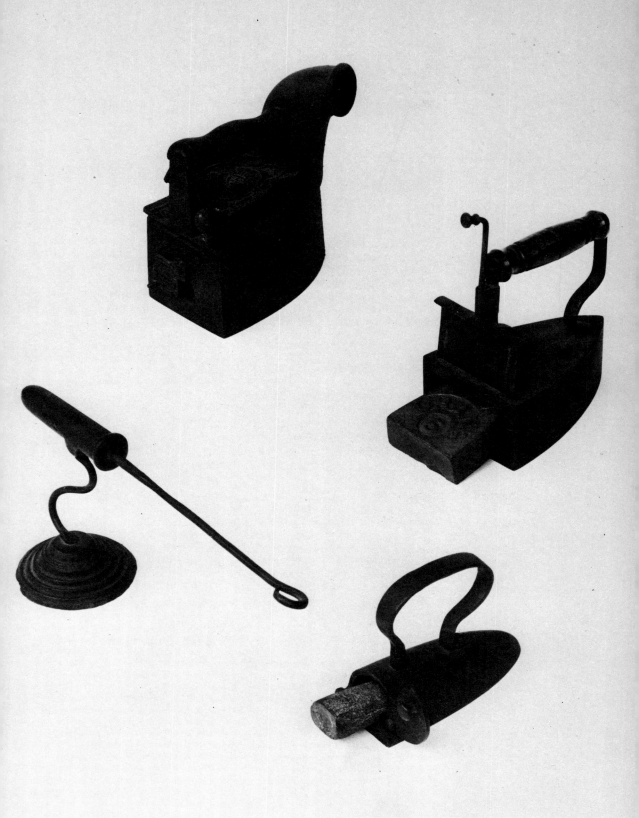

Bibliography

ACTON, E. *Modern Cookery for Private Families*. London, 1845.

AMERICAN HERITAGE EDITORS. *American Heritage Cookbook*. New York, 1969.

AMERICAN HERITAGE EDITORS. *American Heritage Guide to Antiques*. New York, 1970.

BEECHER, C. and STOWE, H. B. *The American Woman's Home*. 1869, reprinted 1972.

BAYNE-POWELL, R. *Housekeeping in the 18th Century*. London, 1956.

BURTON, E. *The Early Victorians at Home*. London, 1972.

COX, W. *Book of Pottery and Porcelain*. New York, 1944.

COYSH, A. W. *Blue and White Transfer Ware and Blue printed Earthenware*. Newton Abbot and Vermont, 1972.

DRUMMOND, J. C. and WILBRAHAM A. *The Englishman's Food*. London and New York, 1939.

EARLE, A. M. *Homelife in Colonial Times*. New York, 1974.

EVAN-THOMAS, O. *Domestic Utensils of Wood*. London, 1932.

GODDEN, G. *Encyclopaedia of British Pottery and Porcelain Marks*. London and New York, 1968.

GODDEN, G. *Illustrated Encyclopaedia of British Pottery and Porcelain*. London and New York, 1966.

HAMILTON, H. *History of the Homeland*. London, 1946.

HARRISON, M. *The Kitchen in History*. London, 1972.

Harrods Catalogue of 1895.

HAYWARD, A. *Colonial lighting*. New York, 1962.

HOUGH, W. *Collection of Heating and Lighting Utensils in the United States*. Washington, 1928.

Ironmongers Trade Gazette.

KAUFFMAN, H. J. *Early American Copper, Tin and Brass*. New York, 1950.

LINDSAY, J. S. *Iron and Brass Implements of the English and American Home*. Boston and London, 1964.

LABAREE, B. W. *The Boston Tea Party*. Oxford and New York, 1968.

O'DEA, W. *Making Fire*. H.M.S.O. London, 1964.

PINTO, E. H. *Treen and other wooden Bygones*. London, 1969.

PHIPPS, F. *Colonial Kitchens and their Gardens*. New York, 1972.

RAMSAY, J. *American Potters and Pottery*. Clinton, Mass., 1939.

SWANK, J. M. *History of the Manufacture of Iron in all Ages*. Philadelphia 1892, reprinted, 1965.

Sears Roebuck Catalogues 1900 and 1902.

WATKINS, C. M. *Artificial Lighting in America*. New York, 1952.

WATKINS, L. W. *Early New England Potters and their Wares*. Hamden, Conn., 1968.

WALKER, R. H. *Everyday Life in the Age of Enterprise*. London, 1968.

WILSON, C. A. *Food and Drink in Britain*. London, 1973.

WRIGHT, L. B. *Everyday Life in Colonial America*. New York, 1966.

Picture acknowledgements

Page numbers given, those in italics refer to colour.

Horsham Museum, Sussex: 13, 55, 59, 65, 99, 107. The Royal Pavilion, Art Gallery and Museums, Brighton: *15*. The Meating Place, Port Washington, New York; Sheila and Daniel Nilva, New York: 17, 51. Science Museum, London, photograph supplied by Cooper Bridgeman Library, London: *19*. Sheila and Daniel Nilva, New York: 21, *23, 69,* 81, *87,* 93, *95.* Then Antiques, Great Neck, New York; Sheila and Daniel Nilva, New York: 25, *27, 53.* Horsham Museum Society, Sussex: 29. Maureen Thompson, London: *31.* Fitzwilliam Museum, Cambridge: *33* (both pictures). Crown copyright, Science Museum, London: 35, *73,* 101. The Meating Place, Port Washington, New York: *37,* 105. Christopher Sykes Antiques, Woburn: *39, 61, 67, 83, 103.* Josiah Wedgwood and Sons Limited, Stoke-on-Trent: 41. Author's collection: 43. Lee Berman, Little Neck, New York; Sheila and Daniel Nilva, New York: 47, *49,* 71, 85. Linda Postan, London: *45.* The Meating Place, Port Washington, New York; Then Antiques, Great Neck, New York; Sheila and Daniel Nilva, New York: *63.* Then Antiques, Great Neck, New York: 75, *79.* Lee Berman, Little Neck, New York: *77.* Lee Berman, Little Neck, New York; Phoebe Phillips, London: 89. Phillips the Auctioneers, London: *91,* 97.

The following photographers were commissioned to take photographs for this book:
A.R. Teugels, Art Camera, Kingston-upon-Thames: 13, 29, *39,* 55, 59, *61,* 65, *67, 83,* 99, *103,* 107.
Otto Maya Studios Inc., New York: 17, 21, *23,* 25, *27, 37,* 47, *49,* 51, *53, 57, 63, 69,* 71, 75, *77, 79,* 81, 85, *87,* 89, 93, *95,* 105.
A.C. Cooper Limited London: *31,* 43, *45, 91,* 97.

Index